Choosing a Jewish Life

Other books by Anita Diamant

Choosing a

Jewish Life

A HANDBOOK FOR
PEOPLE CONVERTING
TO JUDAISM AND FOR
THEIR FAMILY AND FRIENDS

Anita Diamant

SCHOCKEN BOOKS
New York

All rights reserved under International and Pan-American Copyright
Conventions. Published in the United States by Schocken Books Inc., New York,
and simultaneously in Canada by Random House of Canada Limited, Toronto.
Distributed by Pantheon Books, a division of Random House, Inc., New York.
Originally published in hardcover by Schocken Books Inc., New York, in 1997.

Library of Congress Cataloging-in-Publication Data

Diamant, Anita.
Choosing a Jewish life : a handbook for people converting to Judaism
and for their family and friends / Anita Diamant.
p.   cm.
Includes bibliographical references.
ISBN 0-8052-1095-4
1. Proselytes and proselyting, Jewish. I. Title.
BM729.P7D53   1997
296.7'1—dc20   96-32991

Random House Web Address: http://www.randomhouse.com/

Book design by Deborah Kerner

Printed in the United States of America

19 18 17 16 15 14 13

Grateful acknowledgment is made to the following for permission to reprint
previously published and unpublished material:

Janet Berkenfield: "From the Meditation on the Sh'ma" by Janet Berkenfield, from
Siddur Birkat Shalom, published by the Havurat Shalom Siddur Project, Somerville,
Mass. 1993. Reprinted by permission of the author. · Bloch Publishing Company:
"Why I Am a Jew" by Edmund Flegg. Reprinted by permission of Bloch Publishing
Company. · Noa Rachael Kushner: "Meditation Before Mikvah" by Noa Rachael
Kushner. Reprinted by permission of the author. · Jeanne Lovy: March 9, 1991, letter
from Jeanne Lovy to Rabbi David Wolfman. Reprinted by permission of Jeanne
Lovy. · Howard Schwartz and ACUM Ltd.: "Rachel," translated by Naomi Nir, from
Voices Within the Ark, edited by Howard Schwartz, translation copyright © 1980 by
Naomi Nir and Howard Schwartz. Rights in Israel for "Shirat Rahel" by Rahel,
copyright © by Rahel, are administered by ACUM Ltd., Israel. Reprinted by per-
mission of Howard Schwartz and ACUM Ltd. · Danny Siegel: "May Your Eyes
Sparkle" by Danny Siegel from Unlocked Doors (1983); "Above All, Teach This New-
born Child" and "Statement by a Woman Who Has Chosen to Be a Jew" by Danny
Siegel from A Hearing Heart (1992). Reprinted by permission of the author. · Hilary
Tham: "Dayenu" From Bad Names for Women by Hilary Tham (Word Works,
Washington, D.C., 1989). Reprinted by permission of the author. · Wallace Literary
Agency, Inc.: "Sh'ma" by Marge Piercy, from Or Chadash (P'nai Or Siddur), 1989,
copyright © 1989 by Marge Piercy and Middlemarsh, Inc. Reprinted by permission
of the Wallace Literary Agency, Inc.

For my father,
MAURICE DIAMANT,
an eternal optimist
whose memory is a blessing,
and
for my teacher,
RABBI LAWRENCE KUSHNER

A young man studying for conversion turned to his teacher and said, "But, Rabbi Kushner, Fitzpatrick isn't a Jewish name." To which Kushner replied, "It will be."

Contents

CONTENTS

CONTENTS

Acknowledgments

Dr. Judith Himber, Rabbi Larry Kushner, Rabbi Barbara Penzner, Rabbi Carl Perkins, Leslie Tuttle, and Rabbi David Wolfman are thoughtful, wise, generous, and extremely busy people who took the time to read this book, chapter by chapter, as I wrote it. Friends and teachers, they were unfailingly helpful, and their comments made this a far better book.

My research put me in touch with many wonderful people. Thanks to Rabbi Norman J. Cohen and Professor Egon Mayer for sharing their respective passions with me. Thanks also to Drs. Joseph Adolph and Robert Levenson, my *mohelim*. For their contributions, I gratefully acknowledge the help of Elaine Adler, Rabbi Al Axelrad, Rabbi Lewis Barth, Sylvia Beller, Janet Berkenfield, Teddy Bofman, Rabbi Lenore Bohm, Paula Brody, Robin Braverman, Karen Shevet Dinah, Cantor Roy Einhorn, David Fitzpatrick, Rabbi David Gelfand, Rabbi Myron S. Geller of the Gerim Institute, Ellen S. Glazer, Sheila Goldberg, Dru Greenwood, Shoshana Brown Gutoff, Brad Harvey, Pamela Hitchcock, June Andrews Horowitz, Jack Jacobs and Ellen Simpson, Kathy Kahn, Susan Kanoff, Sheila Katz, Susan M. Katz at Stars of David, Rabbi Samuel Kenner, Karen Kushner, Rabbi Steven Kushner, Gila Langner at *Kerem* magazine, Lori and Eric Lass, Marilyn Levenson and Mark McConnell, Susan Leviton, Judith Lytel and Leslie Sternberg, Rabbi Bernard Mehlman, Debra Mikkelson, Rabbi Steven H.

Moskowitz, Dr. Ellen Pashall, Brian Rosman, Rabbi Dennis Sasso, Rabbi Sandy Sasso, Carol Scheingold, Cantor Robert Scherr, Hannah Tiferet Siegel, Rabbi Mark Dov Shapiro, Danny Siegel, Ellen Simpson, Debra Goldstein Smith, Cantor Louise Treitman, Shirley Waxman, Cantor Jennifer Werby, Kai Wilson, Chris and Nancy Winship, Rabbi Paul Yedwed, Cantor Lorel Zar-Zessler and Arnold Zar-Zessler, and Rabbi Elaine Zecher.

I would also like to thank everyone who attended the 1995–96 conversion and outreach discussion groups at Congregation Beth El of the Sudbury River Valley, where I learned many things—especially how little born-Jews understand about the extraordinary experience of choosing Judaism.

Grateful thanks to all of my writing buddies who listened while I kvetched, especially Amy Hoffman, Valerie Monroe, and Edward Myers. Thanks to my agent, Faith Hamlin, and to Arthur H. Samuelson at Schocken Books, who knows what he's doing, and to Jennifer Turvey at Schocken, who made it happen.

My husband, Jim Ball, and my daughter, Emilia, are simply the best cheerleaders a writer ever had.

Preface
My Conversion Story—
and Yours

IT WAS A BEAUTIFUL JUNE MORNING. I WAS SITTING in my car, parked on a residential side street and staring at the doorway of a substantial brick building, which housed the professional office of Dr. Schlossberg, a urologist and *mohel*— someone who performs circumcisions. Jim Ball, my fiancé, had gone through the door a few minutes earlier, accompanied by our rabbi, Lawrence Kushner, to undergo *hatafat dam brit*, the ritual taking of a drop of blood, required by Jewish law of already circumcised male converts.

Nearly three years earlier, when I first fell in love with Jim, I realized that I'd found a life partner, someone with whom I could imagine having a family. At the time, I didn't give a thought to the fact that Jim wasn't Jewish. The issue of "intermarriage" didn't even occur to me, nor did the possibility of conversion. But recognizing the depth of my commitment to Jim made me acutely aware of my own powerful need to transmit a sense of Jewishness to any child we might have together.

Jim, a lapsed Presbyterian, had no objection to the idea of raising Jewish children and he was perfectly willing to help me build a Jewish home. The problem was mine. Not only was I nonobservant and unaffiliated, I had almost no knowledge of the traditions, history, or rituals of my heritage. Exactly what was it that I wanted to pass on to my theoretical children?

On the one hand, I knew myself to be utterly and unconditionally Jewish. My parents were Holocaust survivors, and although there was very little ritual or observance in my childhood and my formal Jewish education was virtually nonexistent, I was raised to be proud of my heritage. However, unlike my parents and grandparents, I could not impart a purely ethnic or historical kind of Jewishness to my child. I would have to teach her how to be a Jew on my own terms. But what were my terms? What kind of Jewishness could I pass on?

In search of answers, I began to study and make a few tentative forays into Jewish practice. Jim not only supported me, he joined me. Together, we learned the blessings for lighting candles on Friday night, and after our Shabbat meal, we took turns reading aloud from Abraham Joshua Heschel's poetic masterpiece, *The Sabbath*. It was Jim who found an advertisement seeking members for a Jewish study group, "no prior knowledge necessary." With that small group of strangers who quickly became friends, we discussed Jewish history, fiction, and theology and began to celebrate Hanukkah and Passover.

When I called Rabbi Kushner to ask him about performing our wedding, he answered by explaining the reasons why he does not officiate at interfaith marriages. And then he said, "But if your fiancé has any interest in talking about the possibility of converting, have him give me a call."

When I repeated Rabbi Kushner's words to Jim, he said, "Give me the phone number."

That was our first "conversation" about conversion. In the process of accompanying me on my search for an authentic Jewish identity, Jim had found a spiritual and communal home for himself as well. And he decided to make it official.

Jim and I met with the rabbi regularly for a year after that, reading the books he assigned and attending an "Introduction to Judaism" course with about a hundred other people. In the small discussion group to which we were assigned, we heard stories about how difficult and even painful conversion to Judaism can be. One ambivalent young woman seemed to be attending simply to please her fiancé, while another woman, who was enthusiastic about becoming Jewish, had to confront rejection by her devout Christian parents. In one married couple, the husband's desire to convert met with strong resistance from his born-Jewish wife.

Jim and I read all the books we could find about converting to Judaism. At the time, there were very few, and while those were encouraging, they were extremely vague on the specifics. Although several more books have been published in the intervening years, none of them go into the detail or depth called for by such a life-transforming event. Indeed, until *Choosing a Jewish Life*, no book about conversion has addressed the pain of putting aside Christmas, or described exactly what happens at the *mikvah*, or at a *hatafat dam brit*.

The door to the brick house finally opened. "It's nothing I ever want to do again," said Jim, with a wince and a grin as we drove to the *mikvah*, where we met Rabbi Kushner and two other rabbis. The three of them comprised the *bet din*, a court of Jewish law convened to evaluate Jim's sincerity and readiness.

The rabbis asked him to talk about his decision to become a Jew and to explain his understanding of Shabbat, the Exodus from Egypt, how he planned to establish a Jewish home. After a spirited fifteen-minute conversation, the rabbis nodded at each other and sent Jim to prepare for *mikvah*.

I stood in the hallway and listened as the rabbi asked Jim if he was ready to enter into the covenant between God and the Jewish people—freely, without reservation, forever, and to the exclusion of all other faiths. Rabbi Kushner's formal voice caromed around the little tiled room. Jim answered "Yes" to every question and recited the blessings for conversion.

A few minutes later, we all walked out into the bright sun. The rabbis embraced Jim warmly. Rabbi Kushner said, "Welcome, brother." Jim's hair was still wet. Neither of us could stop smiling.

The following Shabbat morning, during services at what was now "our" temple, Jim spoke about the journey that brought him to Judaism and about his Hebrew name, which is Jacob. One week later, we were married under a *huppah*— a wedding canopy—made out of a prayer shawl that was my wedding gift to him.

There were really two new-minted Jews under that canopy. Were it not for Jim's conversion I wonder if I would have begun the exploration of Judaism that led me to write books about Jewish weddings, or Jewish baby rituals, or Jewish family life. His decision to become a Jew certainly inspired this book.

Every conversion story is fascinating, unique, precious. Every conversion story is the story of a journey, of a family, of a spiritual quest, of accidents that, in retrospect, don't seem like accidents at all. Because every conversion story is touched by holiness.

Your conversion story is fascinating, unique, precious, and holy. When you become a member of the Jewish people, your story enriches the heritage of the Jewish people. It is a story that will belong to your children if you have children. But your story will also belong to the extended family that is the Jewish people, which will be forever changed by your presence.

If you are reading these words in preparation for your own conversion, I hope *Choosing a Jewish Life* will help you to make your first Jewish choices meaningful and memorable. I hope this book will become a useful part of your own conversion story.

ANITA DIAMANT
Newton, Massachusetts
April 1996—Adar 5756

Choosing a
Jewish Life

Introduction
The Journey to Judaism

*May it be Your will, Adonai, God of our ancestors, to lead
us in peace and guide our steps in safety so that we may
arrive at our destination, alive, happy, and in peace.*

FROM THE BLESSING RECITED BY TRAVELERS
BEFORE EMBARKING ON A JOURNEY

CONVERTING TO JUDAISM IS AN EXTRAORDINARY
journey—a process of study, experimentation, growth, and
self-discovery unlike virtually any other experience. Choosing Judaism means taking yourself outside the mainstream of
American culture and into a parallel universe, where time
moves according to an ancient cyclical rhythm, where familiar
words have different meanings, where spirituality infuses daily
life through blessings for every occasion.

Few people in your life may truly understand how profound, confusing, and beautiful it is to become a Jew. Non-
Jews tend to see conversion as an expression of religious faith,
even though faith, belief, and creed are of secondary importance in Judaism. Born-Jews, on the other hand, tend to

think of conversion solely in terms of family and children, and gloss over the radical spiritual and personal transformation it entails.

Even so, there are many who understand completely. Although accurate statistics are lacking, at least four thousand North Americans convert to Judaism annually—more than at any point in the past two thousand years.[1] Indeed, one out of every thirty-seven[2] American Jews is a Jew-by-choice.

Most converts discover Judaism as a result of falling in love with a Jew. Others find their way through friendships, college courses, and coincidences that, at some point, begin to seem more like signposts than accidents. Regardless of why you started or how far you've traveled, by the time you're reading a book called *Choosing a Jewish Life*, you already know that Judaism is a rich, appealing, and all-embracing way of life. By now, you are probably also aware that becoming a Jew isn't simple or easy because Judaism is so complicated and sometimes even contradictory.

Conversion is an exquisitely personal choice, and while it is not the goal of *Choosing a Jewish Life* to persuade anyone to become Jewish, the underlying assumption in these pages is that you are at least seriously considering the possibility. The "you" in these pages refers to the seeker, the student of Judaism, the Jew-in-process.

However, *Choosing a Jewish Life* does have an agenda. By encouraging you to shape the process of your own conversion, this book hopes to launch you into a lifetime of Jewish decision-making. Because a "Jew-by-choice" is not someone who makes a single major decision called conversion; a Jew-by-choice is someone who makes a home inside the act of Jewish choosing.

This definition is not unique to converts. Every Jew alive today—whether born to Jewish parents or not—is faced with decisions about how to be a Jew and what kind of Jew to be. There are no ghetto walls or quotas anymore, which means that Jews have the option of walking away from Judaism altogether—and some do just that.

Those who identify themselves as Jews are then faced with a selection of several "Judaisms": Conservative, Reconstructionist, Reform, Orthodox—even New Age. To make matters more confusing, there are many Jews who consider themselves secular and avoid affiliating with any movement or synagogue. And to complicate things even further, Jewish choices tend to change over the course of a lifetime. Affiliations change. Observances are embraced, abandoned, and embraced again. Few Jewish decisions are final. A perfectly reasonable answer to a question like "Do you belong to a synagogue?" or "Do you keep kosher?" is, "Not at the moment," or "Not yet."

Choosing is the cornerstone of liberal Judaism, which includes the Conservative, Reconstructionist, and Reform movements. *Choosing a Jewish Life* describes conversion within the framework of liberal, or non-Orthodox, Judaism. Although liberal Jews do have their disagreements, they share the basic assumption that Judaism evolves over time, and that Jews in every generation struggle to reconcile ancient ways with modern challenges. For liberal Jews, *halachah* (Jewish law) is a historical collection of human responses to the divine and thus is open to interpretation and change.[3]

The Orthodox approach to conversion, which is rooted in a more literal understanding of Jewish law, is not included in this book. This is intended not as an insult or a judgment, but simply as a reflection of the gulf that separates the liberal and Orthodox communities on the perennially thorny topic of "who is a Jew." For a comprehensive and welcoming account of Orthodox conversion, see *Becoming a Jew* by Rabbi Maurice Lamm (Jonathan David Publishers, 1991), or contact a local Orthodox rabbi.

Choosing a Jewish Life is divided into six sections, each of which begins with some of the many questions that prospective converts ask. (While Judaism rarely provides simple or unanimous answers, the tradition has an abiding respect for questions and questioners.)

Part I, "Making Your Way," describes conversion as an act of redefinition. When you choose Judaism, familiar words and ideas may assume new and hitherto foreign meanings; the Holocaust, for example, becomes *your* nightmare. Christmas becomes somebody else's holiday. Your decision also redefines your family of origin and your new Jewish family, and it changes things between you and your Jewish partner, too.

Part II, "Preparation," and Part III, "Rituals and Ceremonies," explain the conversion process itself: from selecting a rabbi, to choosing a Hebrew name, to the physical/spiritual gestures of transformation such as *mikvah*. Here you will discover the wealth of Jewish choices open to you from the very beginning of your Jewish life—choices that will enable you to make this life passage meaningful and memorable.

Part IV, "Celebrating Conversion," describes ways to add *simcha*—joy—to the process of becoming a Jew.

Part V, "Becoming Jewish," contains suggestions for ways to find your footing and your spiritual home. Here you will find practical advice about choosing a synagogue, an introduction to performing *mitzvot*, and an invitation to Torah study—one of the great challenges and pleasures of Judaism.

In Part VI, "Your History: A Short History of Conversion to Judaism," you'll find your decision reflected throughout the four-thousand-year saga of the Jewish people.

What's in a Name?

THROUGHOUT *Choosing a Jewish Life*, the terms "convert" and "Jew-by-choice" are used interchangeably. Nobody likes either term very much. As one Jew-by-choice put it, "The word 'convert' always makes me think of a currency exchange." And while "Jew-by-choice" implies a more active stance, it's still a clumsy locution.

In the Bible and in classical Jewish writings, the word for "convert" is *ger*, a word that can also mean "stranger" or "sojourner." "Proselyte" comes from the Greek translation of *ger*, and while its derivation is actually quite nice (from the word *prosēlytos*, "one who has arrived"), it sounds hopelessly quaint. Some people object to any term that singles out converts as a separate category of Jews. Certainly, anyone who chooses Judaism is fully a Jew. Rabbinic tradition forbade making an issue or even mention of any convert's origin for fear that born-Jews would lord it over those who began life as pagans. Today, however, "convert," "Jew-by-choice," *ger*, and "prose-lyte" are anything but insults. Within the pages of this book, they are honorific titles, a way to show respect—indeed, they are terms of endearment.

As a Jew-by-choice, you inherit four thousand years of Jewish history, which is not just an academic or esoteric pursuit but a living presence. Self-conscious echoes of the Jewish past—from ancient Palestine, medieval Spain, and nineteenth-century Poland—suffuse contemporary Jewish prayer, study, and even the rhythm of the year. The Jewish calendar is studded with holidays that recall and, at Passover especially, reenact the past. The sanctification of history is an ongoing process for Jews, which is why, in 1951, the observance of Yom HaShoah (Holocaust Remembrance Day) became a permanent memorial to the six million Jews murdered by the Nazis.

"A people's memory is its history," wrote Yiddish author Isaac Leib Peretz, "and like a person without a memory, so a people without a history cannot grow wiser or better." Finding your place within Jewish history is a way to find roots as a Jew and to imagine yourself into the future of the Jewish people.

All of Jewish history is the heritage of every Jew, but just as Jews from Brooklyn seek out and swap stories from the old neighborhood, just as Jewish physicians are intrigued by the medical career of the twelfth-century physician-philosopher Moses Maimonides, the history of conversion to Judaism is uniquely yours. Everyone who converted before you is, in a sense, your spiritual ancestor.

The continuous presence of converts through Jewish history is not widely known; it is a "counterhistory," a largely undocumented but essential strand of life, like Jewish women's history, which rarely surfaces in the official chronicles of exiles and rabbis. The history of conversion is, however, present in every retelling of the Jewish past. It can be traced through rabbinical writings on how and why proselytes are to be accepted; it is documented in the names of those who are remembered as converts; and it is evident in the physical and racial diversity of the Jewish people.

Actually, Jews-by-choice bear an obvious and an intimate connection to the very beginning of Jewish history in their names. When you become a Jew, you will be asked to choose a Hebrew name, but you will also automatically "inherit" the names of the father and mother of the entire Jewish people, Abraham and Sarah—neither of whom was born to Jewish parents either.*

Like virtually all other aspects of Judaism, conversion has changed over the past four thousand years: from simple assimilation into Israelite culture, to a short-lived period of active and successful proselytizing, to centuries when converts posed a mortal danger to Jewish communities and were suspected and even feared. The contemporary welcome for converts represents both a new chapter in Jewish history and a

---

*For example, if you take the Hebrew name Rachel, you become Rachel bat Avraham Avienu v'Sarah Imenu—Rachel the daughter of Abraham our Father and Sarah our Mother. See "Choosing a Hebrew Name."

return to the very beginning of Jewishness, to Abraham and Sarah and the souls who accompanied them, leaving the world of their parents to make history.

No one really knows how many people are converting to Judaism today, but the numbers are more significant than they have been for nearly two thousand years. Jews-by-choice are literally changing the face of American Jewry. The Jewish community has been caught by surprise at this infusion of new energy and commitment, and is sometimes unprepared to greet converts with the information and welcome they need and deserve.

Choosing a Jewish Life was written to help fill that gap and to make your experience of conversion as meaningful and joyful as possible by providing information, resources, suggestions, and, above all, welcome.

In the daily worship liturgy, the series of ancient Hebrew prayers called the Amidah asks God to bestow "tender mercies" on the people of Israel. The Amidah singles out certain groups for God's special attention: these include the pious, the elders, and righteous proselytes.

Like you.

PART I

Making

Your

Way

What does it mean to be part of a "tribe" in a post-tribal world?

Is it fair for me to put my children at risk of anti-Semitism?

Why is it so important to my partner that I convert since he never sets foot in a synagogue?

If I convert, why won't all Jews recognize my children as Jews?

Will I ever feel any connection to the state of Israel?

Why does the idea of having a Christmas tree make my wife so crazy?

How do I tell my parents I'm not going to take communion anymore?

Why don't we talk about God more in my conversion class?

Can I go through with this even if I have doubts?

Should I ask my children to convert, too?

*T*HERE ARE MANY GATES INTO THE HOUSE OF Israel. The tradition suggests that there are 613 entrances—one for each of the commandments contained in the Torah. But there are probably as many reasons for choosing Judaism as there are people who have chosen.

The expected answers—"I'm marrying a Jew" or "We want to give our children a single, clear religious identity"—don't begin to tell the whole story of why anyone converts to Judaism.

"I can't say that I would be converting if I hadn't met my fiancée. She's certainly the reason I got into studying and taking the 'Introduction to Judaism' course. But I am not converting for her. That would be hypocritical and hollow. She introduced me to Judaism, but I'm converting for me."

"I'm a Jew because of my children who are Jews. I wanted to stand on the *bimah* during my older daughter's bat mitzvah and hand her the Torah. It meant a lot to her, and it meant a lot to me, too. It was a great moment for all of us."

You may not be able to articulate all of the reasons you're thinking about converting. You may even be embarrassed by some of them. Perhaps part of your decision has to do with the way that the melodies of Hebrew prayers move you to tears. Maybe it has something to do with how your Jewish in-laws have made you a part of their family. Or perhaps it was the way that the moon shone on your face in the temple *sukkah*, last autumn.

"Shabbat converted me. When my wife and I decided to marry, I thought that we'd just join a Unitarian church, where we could celebrate all kinds of holidays. But the rituals and rest and beauty of Shabbat—the wisdom of Shabbat—made me want to be a Jew."

Life is lived in details, in momentary flashes of revelation, in relationships that ebb and flow. And yet, trying to explain the importance of those details and flashes seems nearly impossible.

"I converted really because of a class I took in college. A Jewish professor of religion at my Catholic women's college opened the Bible and started talking about it in a way that blew me away. Suddenly, there was room for me in the Bible. I couldn't get enough of the Torah."

"I'm converting because Judaism is a way of life. It's not a once-a-week visit to a building, but an everyday thing. I want to be a Jew so that my dining room table will be an altar. Because as Jews, it's what I do—everything I do—that matters."

Nobody makes a choice as life-altering as this without some trepidation, some ambivalence. Choosing Judaism means rejecting other paths and putting some distance between you and your family of origin. And yet, doubt is a normal part of change. Brides and grooms have passing bouts of cold feet.

Pregnant women who always longed to be mothers sometimes wonder if they've made a terrible mistake. Having moments of worry (or even panic) about what you're doing doesn't mean you're unworthy or unprepared—only that you're human.

"It's like I'm starting on a trip and I'm not sure where it's going to take me. I keep asking the rabbi when I'll know I'm ready. But he says I'm as ready as I'm ever going to be."

New Definitions

BECOMING A JEW IS AN ACT OF DEFINITION and redefinition. You rename yourself as a Jew with a new Hebrew name. You're asked to master new concepts and foreign words: *mitzvah*, Torah, *tzedakah, mikvah*. Even more confusing, you must learn new meanings for long-familiar terms because words you've heard and spoken since childhood don't mean the same things to Jews and to non-Jews. For instance, Christians and Jews don't understand the word "faith" in the same way at all, and the Jewish notion of "peoplehood" really has no cognate among non-Jews.

While *tzedakah* is often translated as "charity," the voluntary, from-the-heart quality usually associated with "charity" is very different from the obligation set out in Jewish law—the requirement to help others. Indeed, the notion of "law" itself has a very different Jewish connotation, resting not on a civil code enforced by the state but on a whole legal/moral system called *halachah*, which is mandated by a much higher authority.*

Even to speak of "Judaism" as a religion is problematic. Prior to the nineteenth century, Jews had no way of thinking of their religious practice as separable from every other aspect of daily life. Even today, Judaism defies definition as a religion pure and simple. Unlike other religions, Judaism is also a discreet civilization and culture. The Jews have been called a nation, a tribe, a race, a folk, an ethnic group, and the "people of the book." Jewish tradition makes reference to the house of Israel, and to the people Israel.

"Jews are a people," writes Julius Lester, a convert to Judaism. "They are of many nationalities and tongues—atheists, agnostic, and some who practice Zen meditation and chant Buddhist mantras and sing Hindu hymns. Yet they are Jews. That is what is so confusing to others about being Jewish. It is not a belief system or even subscribing to a particular religious practice. It is belonging to a people, not only those living but also those who are not."[1]

℘eoplehood

ℬECOMING A JEW means attaching yourself to four thousand years of history, to a complex literature, to a brand of humor, even to certain foods. Becoming an American Jew

---

*Except in Israel, where the civic law and Jewish law are intertwined. See later in this chapter, "Israel."

means acquiring a relationship to at least two foreign languages: Hebrew and Yiddish. Converting to Judaism means learning what to do in a synagogue, how to send and receive the verbal and nonverbal cues that signal Jewishness, getting the jokes. Being a Jew asks you to subsume a part of your individuality into the larger, corporate experience of the Jewish people.

Talking about "peoplehood" at the dawn of the twenty-first century may seem like an anachronism. After all, this is the age of the global village, knit together by instant communications, international travel, and mass culture. The alternative to a totally homogenized life on a shrinking planet is usually thought of in terms of radical individualism and personal freedom. But that philosophy tends to produce loneliness, isolation, and a hunger to belong to something larger and more durable than oneself. Becoming a member of the Jewish people is one way to satisfy that hunger because it gives individuals access to deep wells of continuity and community that transcend time and space.

For most human beings, family provides the anchor of belonging, recognition, and love, and family is the paradigm for Jewish peoplehood. Just as families share values, the Jewish people shares a set of life-affirming values. Just as there is a sense of personal continuity for people who live to see their grandchildren grow up, so do Jews feel invested in a Jewish future that includes and transcends the lives of a single nuclear family. Becoming Jewish can provide a tangible sense of eternity—not necessarily in an afterlife but within the realm of human life and the confines of this world.

Even so, the profound difference between converting to a religion called Judaism and joining the Jewish people is difficult to grasp because there is little that obviously distinguishes most Jews from most non-Jews in America today. Jews and non-Jews speak the same language, wear the same clothes, attend the same colleges, listen to the same music. And yet, there *is* an "us-and-them" aspect to being a Jew. Even the most assimilated fifth-generation American Jew feels a sense of "otherness" in America, which is unselfconsciously suffused with Christian assumptions and symbols: from the fact that Sunday is the official Sabbath, to the mass-marketing of Christmas and Easter. On the other hand, Jews tend to feel a connection to total strangers who happen to be Jewish, and when Jews travel outside their own country, they often will visit Jewish neighborhoods and historical sites, seeking out other members of the global family.[2]

Who Is a Jew? Part 1

In America, religious affiliation is an expression of personal identity. In a nation without identity cards that declare you "Christian," "Muslim," or "Jew," you are who and what you say you are.

But it is not that simple among Jews. Since Judaism's legal system is integral and essential, religious status is a legal matter, which has precipitated some nasty disputes about who is and who isn't a Jew. Unfortunately, Jews-by-choice find themselves at the center of one of Jewish history's more rancorous "who is a Jew" arguments.

Basically, the crux of the problem rests on differing views of *halachah,* or traditional Jewish law. According to *halachah,* any person born to a Jewish mother is a Jew. Jewish law also mandates the process of conversion, which includes the rabbinically supervised rituals of immersion and circumcision, and a sincere commitment to follow the *mitzvot,* the Torah's commandments. Liberal Jews view *halachah* as an evolving human system that has and should change in response to history. Thus, the Conservative, Reconstructionist, and Reform movements have modified the legal requirements for conversion to greater and lesser degrees, although all do have standards and rules.[3]

Orthodox Jews, on the other hand, tend to treat *halachah* as God-given, so that substantial changes to the law—in the absence of Orthodox rabbinic rulings—are not acceptable. In the Orthodox community, people converted under Conservative, Reconstructionist, or Reform auspices are not considered Jewish.

In order to avoid any challenge to their authenticity as Jews, some prospective converts seek out Orthodox rabbis in the hope of undergoing a conversion that will satisfy the requirements of the entire Jewish world.[4] But while there are notable exceptions, the Orthodox rabbinate is not eager to work with converts, and many Orthodox rabbis discourage prospective candidates from even trying.[5]

While this debate may be disheartening for prospective Jews, it's important to remember that you choose *a* Judaism when you choose to become a Jew. Judaism is not (nor has it ever been) a monolithic religion; there is no Vatican, no universal catechism. A liberal conversion will make you a liberal Jew, which is to say, a Jew who makes choices. Becoming a liberal Jew means understanding that while you may violently disagree with the beliefs and practices of some forms of Orthodox Judaism, Orthodox Jews are your cousins—distant and perhaps even hostile cousins—but relatives nonetheless.

The debate around legal status is especially acute in Israel, where people do carry identity cards and personal status is legally supervised by the Orthodox rabbinate.* Prospective converts studying with liberal rabbis are often warned that their status as Jews may not be recognized in Israel or that they may not be permitted to immigrate there as Jews; these are matters to discuss with your rabbi.

Who Is a Jew? Part 2

IN SOME WAYS, converts offer a new answer to the age-old question "Who is a Jew?" Your very existence—both as an individual Jew-by-choice and as part of a historic influx of new Jews—challenges deeply held but unexamined assump-

---

* In the state of Israel, the Orthodox rabbinate exercises legal control over issues of personal status including marriage and divorce—for Jewish citizens. It is a misconception that Jews-by-choice whose conversions are supervised by non-Orthodox rabbis are not permitted to immigrate to Israel. According to the Israeli Law of Return, citizenship is automatically granted to all Jews who seek it—without regard to affiliation. If you are a Jew-by-choice who converted under Reform or Conservative auspices and eventually "make aliyah" (move to Israel), you will be issued an identity card that declares you a Jew.

   However, you will face problems in Israel if, for example, you wish to get married. At that point, all converts have to prove their Jewishness according to Orthodox standards in order to have a state-sanctioned wedding.[6]

tions about Jewish identity or Jewish*ness*—also called Yiddishkeit. Which is one reason why some born-Jews may have difficulty accepting you as a "real" Jew.

Many nonobservant or unaffiliated American Jews define themselves as members of an ethnic group. Ethnicity—a sense of transcendent cultural kinship—is certainly an important part of the Jewish experience. Jews still try to recognize one another by looking at noses and last names. In the conversational gambit called "Jewish geography," Jews from different parts of the country (or planet) try to figure out how they are connected by blood, marriage, affiliation, or acquaintance. There are still foods, jokes, and patterns of speech that "read" Jewish.

But Jewish ethnicity has been declining for a long time. Intermarriage has played a part in the change, but it is not the only reason for the fading of Yiddishkeit and the assimilation of American Jewry. For the most part, American Jews long ago abandoned the urban neighborhoods that supported a unique cultural identity. Outside of a few Orthodox strongholds, American Jews know only a handful of Yiddish words. Jewish community centers devote much more money and space to sports facilities than to Jewish culture or study.

No one needs to convert to Judaism in order to eat bagels or read Philip Roth or "get" Billy Crystal's Jewish jokes. Most Jews-by-choice are religious seekers who are attracted to Judaism because of the way it wrestles with God, and/or because Judaism identifies the home as a sanctuary, and/or because of the fact that the synagogue is a center of learning as well as worship. For nonobservant, unaffiliated, or secular born-Jews whose religious education stopped at the age of thirteen, the spiritual curiosity and religious openness of Jews-by-choice challenge all kinds of assumptions about what it means to be a Jew.

Jews-by-choice present a new paradigm for all Jews. In terms of ethnicity, Irish-American Jews, African-American Jews, Italian-American Jews, and Japanese-American Jews are redefining the Jewish nose, the Jewish menu, the Jewish name. And for liberal Jews, converts pose an even more fundamental challenge. The Jew-by-choice embodies the fact that it is no longer possible to simply *be* Jewish in an unselfconscious, effortless ethnic way. An authentic sense of being Jewish—of Jewish*ness*—is available only to those who live as Jews, who *do* Jewish. Fortunately, the list of Jewish things to do is enormous and its variety (study, prayer, affiliation, ritual practice, social activism, music, hospitality, philanthropy, cooking) encourages individuality as much as it fosters community.

In a world where Jews participate fully in the free marketplace of ideas, in a time when ghetto walls and anti-Semitic quotas do not exist, in a time of spiritual hunger, converts are a contemporary model of Jewish identity. From synagogue pulpits of every denomination, the message has been repeated so often it has become a truism: "Whether we are born Jewish or have converted to Judaism, we are all Jews-by-choice."

Chosenness

THE IDEA that God chose the Jews is an ancient belief that poses an enormous philosophical problem for all Jews. Although Judaism is a deeply democratic tradition—believing in the universal brotherhood/sisterhood of humanity—the idea of chosenness seems to divide the world into "us" and "them," with the Jewish "us" having a special, if not superior, relationship to God.

Jews have never believed themselves possessed of the only "true" faith or exclusive pathway to God, which is why Judaism was never a missionary religion. Since the rabbis taught that all the righteous among the nations could attain "the world to come," there was no need to save the souls of non-Jews; their own religions gave them access to the Holy One and to salvation. Nevertheless, the idea of a special relationship between God and the Jews is a central tenet of Judaism. The Shema, the quintessential statement of Jewish theology, is preceded in the prayer book by the phrase "You have chosen us from all the peoples and nations and associated us with Your great name."[7]

Abraham Joshua Heschel, one of the great rabbis and teachers of the twentieth century wrote, "The idea of a chosen people does not suggest the preference for a people based upon a discrimination among a number of peoples. We do not say that we are a superior people. The 'chosen people' means a people approached and chosen by God. The significance in this term is genuine in relation to God rather than in relation to other peoples. It signifies not a quality inherit in the people but a relationship between the people and God."[8]

Nevertheless, Jews clung to the idea of chosenness as a kind of psychospiritual life raft—especially in times of severe persecution. Chosenness helped an oppressed people maintain a sense of their value and worth by exalting the sufferers and demeaning their persecutors. It also prompted a fair amount of self-deprecating humor. According to one old Yiddish saw, "Thou hast chosen us from amongst all the nations—so why did you have to pick on the Jews?"

The rabbinic tradition rarely connects the idea of chosenness to superiority; indeed, the rabbis believed that God laid far heavier responsibilities upon the Jews than the other peoples of the world by giving them the Torah. Nevertheless, the idea of chosenness remained a source of pride and ethnocentrism among Jews for centuries and is, in fact, still part of the Jewish psyche. But only part. The ethic of universal brotherhood and justice is an equally unshakable cornerstone of Jewish belief and action. As Jews have become less embattled, less persecuted, and more secure, the need for a narrow, self-aggrandizing sense of chosenness has faded.

Today, the phrase "the chosen people" is often paired with its complement, "the people who chose." This is not a modern idea; according to one traditional interpretation, or *midrash*, the Hebrews were not even God's first choice as recipients of the Torah. God went to several other nations first, asking if they would accept God's covenant. But the other peoples found God's requirements too arduous. When the

Hebrews said yes to God—when they entered into the mutual relationship of covenant—the Torah was given to humanity through the choosing/chosen people who accepted it.[9]

Becoming a Jew means choosing to enter into that covenant through which, in turn, God chooses you. It is a mutual, voluntary embrace.

Faith

CONVERTS to any religious tradition are a special breed of seekers, alive to their own spiritual thirst, eager to find a spiritual home. But prospective Jews are often confused or disappointed by the relative lack of attention paid to faith and belief among born-Jews. Even the process of conversion—the classes, books, and discussions—tends to focus on observance and peoplehood rather than on theology.

The issue of faith gets back to the question of who is a Jew and the fact that belief in God has never been a basis for determining Jewishness. There is no Jewish creed or catechism, and faith has never been a litmus test. Jews, as a matter of birth, simply inherit a tradition that locates them within a covenant with God. If a born-Jew rejects the idea that the covenant includes a Divine Partner, he or she is still part of the agreement. According to some traditionalists, even Jews who convert to Christianity remain Jews—apostate Jews, but Jews nonetheless.

For most non-Jews converting to Judaism, however, faith is a necessary question. Historically, of course, belief in God's existence was integral to Jewish life, language, and culture. But in the modern era, God became an open question rather than the source of all answers for Jews. After the Holocaust, belief seemed nearly impossible for much of a generation.

In America, the land of unprecedented opportunity and secularism, liberal Jews turned away from God and focused on the more tangible aspects of Jewishness, such as social justice, ethnicity, and community. In the wake of the Holocaust, survival itself seemed a sacred calling, and supporting the state of Israel became a primary expression of Jewish life.

Of course, not all liberal Jews stopped believing in, praying to, or writing about God. The 1970s brought a rediscovery of Judaism's spiritual foundations, particularly in the writings of Martin Buber and Abraham Joshua Heschel. Jewish ritual life began to be revived and reshaped. Today, the vitality of liberal Jewish religiosity is evident in the annual publication of scores of new books about contemporary Jewish theology and mysticism. Renewed enthusiasm for traditional forms of study, prayer, and observance exist side by side with new forms of Jewish spiritual practice informed by feminism and various schools of meditation. The religious energy and enthusiasm of Jews-by-choice are part of the "re-sacralization" of liberal Judaism, sometimes called the Jewish renewal movement.

Although faith and belief continue to be open questions in the liberal Jewish world, it is a good time to be a religious seeker in that world. On the occasion of her conversion, Mary Russell wrote, "Judaism has allowed me to lay down my intellectual defenses and to stand, unprotected by cynicism, before the idea of a God who cares passionately about the human moral drama and gives it meaning by remembering our actions and our choices."[10]

Holocaust

A HOLOCAUST is a great fire, a conflagration that consumes. When you become a Jew, this word can no longer be generic. It becomes a proper noun that describes one singular event: the Nazi slaughter of six million Jews and two million other human beings. In converting to Judaism, you make the Holocaust your own personal nightmare. One woman who was studying for conversion told her discussion group that she had been having terrible dreams about Nazis pursuing her. "What right do I have to subject any children I might have to that kind of danger?" she asked.

The Talmud asked a similar question hundreds of years ago: "What reason have you for desiring to become a proselyte? Do you not know that the Jews at the present time are persecuted and oppressed, despised, harassed, and overcome by afflictions?"[11]

Becoming a Jew means voluntarily putting yourself—and your children—on the short end of a very long and dangerous stick. Although institutional, legal, and cultural anti-Semitism has diminished to a remarkable extent in twentieth-century America, prejudice against Jews is not a disease against which the world has been inoculated. Every year, swastikas are painted on synagogue doors, Jewish cemeteries are desecrated, and revisionist historians publish claims that the Nazi Holocaust was a story invented by Jews to reap the sympathy of the world. Jewish children are still asked by their playmates why they killed Christ, and jokes about greedy, selfish, and sexually repressed Jewish-American Princesses still make the rounds.

As a Jew-by-choice, you become vulnerable to a form of bigotry to which you were previously immune. You are also likely to become even more sensitive to all forms of prejudice and discrimination. It is no accident that Jews are statistically overrepresented in social action organizations since Judaism demands *tzedek*—justice—for all people.

But anti-Semitism has not only consigned Jews to flames. It has been a refining fire as well. A story is told about Louis Brandeis (1856–1941), who was a student at Harvard Law School at a time when there were explicit limits on what Jews could hope to achieve. Quotas were in effect and many law offices were completely closed to Jewish attorneys. When Brandeis was in school, his colleagues would say, "Brandeis, you're brilliant. If you weren't a Jew, you could end up on the Supreme Court. Why don't you convert? Then all of your problems would be solved."

Brandeis did not respond to such comments, but on the occasion of his official introduction to an exclusive honor society at the law school, Brandeis took the podium and announced, "I am sorry I was born a Jew." His words were greeted with enthusiastic applause, shouts, and cheers. But when the noise died down he continued. "I'm sorry I was born a Jew, but only because I wish I had the privilege of choosing Judaism on my own."

The initial response of stunned silence slowly gave way to awed applause. Ultimately, his anti-Semitic peers rose and gave him a standing ovation.[12] In 1916, Louis Brandeis became the first Jew appointed to the United States Supreme Court.

Israel

BECOMING A JEW means that Israel belongs to you, just as the Torah and Shabbat belong to you. But it's no easy matter forging a genuine connection to an adoptive spiritual homeland in an unseen and embattled nation on the other side of the planet. And it's not simple resolving the question of dual loyalties once you are, potentially at least, a citizen of that country.

Of course, Israel is more than a small nation in the Middle East. The land of Israel is embedded in four thousand years of Jewish life. In Genesis and throughout the Torah, Israel was the land that God promised and the Jewish people sought, longed for, settled, fought over, were exiled from, and returned to. In every generation since the destruction of the Jewish state during the first century C.E.,* Jews in the Diaspora turned their bodies toward Israel when they prayed. Israel was a place to send *tzedakah*, and the destination for Jewish pilgrims. Israel was a name for the dream of redemption from the suffering of life in Diaspora.

The Zionist movement of the nineteenth century sought to turn what had been a religious goal of redemption and salvation into a political safe haven for world Jewry. That goal was only realized in 1948, after the Holocaust had wiped out one third of the world's Jewish population. The nations of the

---

*Jews use C.E. (Common Era) and B.C.E. (before the Common Era) rather than the designations A.D. and B.C., which refer to the divinity of Jesus (anno domini means "in the year of our Lord").

earth had denied asylum to hundreds of thousands of Jews who escaped but were sent back to Germany to die. The state of Israel was founded amid cries of "Never again," and the first act of the newly created state was the enactment of a "Law of Return," which grants citizenship and safe harbor to all Jews, everywhere.[13]

Today, of course, Israel is a modern state as well as a metaphor for redemption and safety. At Passover, when Jews end the seder with the traditional statement "Next year in Jerusalem," the words conjure up real memories as well as a dream of peace. For Jews who have visited or lived in Israel's capital city, "Next year in Jerusalem" calls to mind memories of sunlight on the city's renowned limestone and a particular feeling of being at home.

For Jews-by-choice, and indeed for Diaspora Jews in general, visiting the land of Israel is really the only way to create a personal connection to *Eretz Yisrael*—the land of Israel. A first trip to Israel is inevitably a watershed Jewish experience, which includes awe at the physical beauty and historical resonance of the place, and an ineffable sense of confirmation in knowing that nearly everyone else on the street—including the taxi driver and the garbage collector—is a Jew, too.

But it's not all sweetness and light. The status of liberal Jewish converts in Israel (and of liberal Judaism) has long been a source of dismay to many American Jews. Furthermore, the actions and embattled politics of the country have occasioned pain, and even outrage, among some Jews. However, even when ties are strained, the connection remains undeniable.

Holidays—Especially Christmas

ON ONE LEVEL, it may seem obvious that choosing Judaism means that you no longer celebrate Christian holidays. Jews-by-choice are often delighted by the number and variety of home-based Jewish holidays. However, for many converts, giving up Christmas is the most significant loss in choosing Judaism.

Not celebrating Christmas—and, if it was a major holiday in your family of origin, Easter—is a radical act of self-redefinition that can feel like a total rejection of your family, your past, and a great deal of who you are. Few born-Jews fully understand how much Christmas may be intimately connected to the earliest and happiest of childhood memories and a living symbol of parental love.

Whether or not it is celebrated as a religious holiday, most non-Jews experience December 25 as the quintessential American celebration of family, wrapped up in twinkling lights, redolent with favorite foods and aromas, resounding with some of the world's best-loved music—everything from Handel's *Messiah* to "Silver Bells."

While some Jews-by-choice declare themselves glad to be relieved of the pressure to live up to a Norman Rockwell–like image of family harmony, for most people, redefining Christmas as "someone else's holiday" takes many years.

Your born-Jewish partner may have no idea what Christmas means to you, and may even view the holiday from a polar-opposite perspective. In December, Jews tend to become acutely aware of themselves as outsiders. Jewish children, in particular, know that the bright lights and the spangled trees are somehow off limits to them. Although America's consumer culture has tried to make Hanukkah into a Jewish version of Christmas, it remains a modest festival of candle-lighting and potato pancake–frying. There is just no contest. The power of Christmas is simply overwhelming.

While a Christmas tree may be nothing more than a pagan symbol of life in your eyes, when your Jewish partner looks at a Christmas tree, he or she may be seeing a symbol of two thousand years of virulent persecution by Christians against Jews. Although anti-Semitism does not loom as a present danger today, its vicious and persistent history has left deep wounds on the Jewish psyche. For some Jews, Christmas reveals the scars.*

Sometimes, however, virulent resistance to Christmas cookies and mistletoe may seem confusing or even hypocritical, especially if your spouse or Jewish friends hung stockings and decorated "Hanukkah bushes" as children. And although it is increasingly rare, some Jews still hang wreaths and exchange gifts on December 25.

Rabbis are emphatic and virtually unanimous in their feeling that there is no place for Christmas celebrations within a Jewish home. It often helps to talk to other Jews-by-choice, to find out how they came to terms with what is often dubbed "the December Dilemma"; congregational Outreach or Keruv committees often sponsor discussion groups around the winter holidays to facilitate just such a conversation.†

---

*For an excellent overview of the emotional legacy of anti-Semitism, see "Jewish-Christian History: A Legacy of Pain," in The Intermarriage Handbook: A Guide for Jews and Christians by Judy Petsonk and Jim Remsen (William Morrow, 1988).

†For a discussion of celebrating Christmas with non-Jewish relatives, see the chapter "Your First Year as a Jew."

Family Matters

WHEN YOU BECOME A JEW, THE REDEFINITION does not end with you. You transform your family of origin into an interfaith family. And if you are marrying or married to a born-Jew, your partner's family likewise acquires a set of non-Jewish relatives and the interfaith label.*

It's hard to predict the reaction to news of your conversion—on either home front. Some families are delighted, some are dismayed. Some open their arms, some turn a cold shoulder. Whatever the initial reaction, it may help you to recall that even eagerly awaited transitions like weddings tend to make families act a little crazy. But unlike the stresses asso-

---

*All references to marriage and spouses refer both to the legal institution of marriage and to committed partnerships that do not have legal sanction, including gay and lesbian couples.

ciated with more conventional passages—like getting married or having a baby—conversion lands you in the middle of largely uncharted waters. There are no glossy magazines called "Modern Convert" with special articles addressed to "The Mother of the New Jew-by-Choice." Nevertheless, other people have been down this road before you; their support and example can make an enormous difference.

Honoring Your Mother and Father

MOM. DAD. We need to talk."*

For many Jews-by-choice, the prospect of this conversation is the most daunting aspect of conversion, and with good reason; all family ties are deep and complicated and many are tightly knotted. Some people wait to convert until after their parents die. Others keep the fact that they have become Jews a secret for years—decades even.

"It would have killed her," they explain. "It would only break his heart."

Some devoutly religious parents respond to the news of conversion with dismay and genuine fear for the immortal souls of their child and grandchildren. Secular parents, on the other hand, may be bewildered that a child of theirs would make any religious commitment at all. Then again, families can surprise you with unexpected support. Some Christians express relief and joy that a previously unchurched son or

_____

*Although much of this section focuses on relationships between parents and children, the same process and conversations may take place with other family members and close friends.

daughter has found a spiritual home in Judaism, and many parents respect the convert's desire to give his or her children an unambiguous religious identity. Still, telling your family that you are becoming a Jew is rarely an easy conversation. However and whenever you decide to deliver the news, remember that your parents will need time to adjust to the idea. Just as becoming a Jew is a process that unfolds over months and years (both before and after the formal ceremonies), becoming an interfaith family takes time, too. Telling your parents that you're going to convert is just the beginning. You will be explaining the meaning and implications of your choice for years to come because your parents will be coming to terms with having a Jewish child—and perhaps Jewish grandchildren—for the rest of their lives.

There is no "right" way or time to tell your parents about your decision. However, psychologists who work with converts suggest that it's better to give your family some time to grow accustomed to the idea. If you present them with a fait accompli ("I'm becoming a Jew next week"), they are likely to feel shut out, cut off, and hurt.

If possible, let your family in on your decision-making process. Tell them you've been celebrating Jewish holidays with your fiancé's family. Let your parents know when you've signed up for an "Introduction to Judaism" course, and talk to them about what you're learning and thinking. Then, when you tell them that you've decided Judaism is right for you, it won't come like a bolt out of the blue.

Given the geographical distance that divides so many families, many converts begin the process by letter. A long, thoughtful letter has the advantage of giving you time to choose your words carefully; it also permits your family time to think about their reply.

If you decide to make an announcement in person, do it in a private and neutral setting rather than at a family celebration or holiday party. Even if you're fairly confident that your family will be supportive and even if you've been preparing them for years, it still may come as a shock. The last thing you want is for your Jewishness to be associated with the time you "ruined" your parents' anniversary dinner.

While there are exceptions, this is a conversation best had without your Jewish partner in the room. It's not fair to put him or her in the middle, especially if your family harbors any suspicion that you're converting "for" him or under pressure from his family.

Matters of faith and religious identity are not easy to discuss. Religion is a taboo subject for many people precisely because it's so easy to give and take offense. When you tell your family you plan to become a Jew, you break this taboo wide open. Matters of faith can become the subject of a heated debate in which people (including you) may be offended or hurt. However, questions are not necessarily insults or attacks. Since it's likely that your parents and other family members will be genuinely curious about your decision, it may be a good idea to plan how to answer such questions as: "Are you converting just to please her (or him)?" "Why can't he (or she) be the one to convert?" "Since when do you believe in God? That's not something we taught you." "But you love Christmas!"

Some rabbis say that they consider these kinds of conversations to be a legitimate test of a prospective Jew's readiness and sincerity. If you can't explain yourself to your parents or remain firm in your resolve when challenged, you may not be ready to convert.

Even if they have no theological objections to your choice, family members—especially parents—may perceive your decision to convert as a rejection of them and everything they believe in. Although all parents have to let go of their children and accept their independence, religious conversion is an unexpected form of separation. It is a declaration of difference that may engender fears of abandonment, loss, or betrayal—even if those words are never spoken. Your family may worry what your becoming Jewish will do to your relationship with them, and wonder what it means for you to become one of "them" rather than one of "us."

You can help reassure your parents by stressing the ties that will always bind you together. Many converts tell their parents that the religious education and moral example they received as children started them on the path that led to this unexpected but fulfilling destination. The decision to become a Jew is thus a continuation of the values and spiritual roots learned from parents. The bottom line is that while you may be choosing a different religion, you are not converting out of your family.

Regardless of your reassurances, however, your conversion may hurt or anger your parents, and their feelings may cause you to respond with strong emotions of your own. When there is acrimony or an outright break, it helps to remember that hurt feelings usually mend. Some parents need a period to mourn, adjust, and make peace with the idea. Sometimes the anger is short-lived, but there are cases where it takes years before a reconciliation is possible. It is up to you to keep the lines of communication open.

Every family is different. In some households, intimate conversations are completely taboo and there may be little or no discussion of your decision. There are families where conversion becomes the focus of unrelated and long-standing family issues. And sometimes converts confront the painful fact that members of their immediate family harbor anti-Semitic stereotypes about Jews and Judaism. If that is the case, it's important to gently but emphatically confront bigotry whenever it arises: "I can't believe you said that, Mom. You raised me to believe in the brotherhood of man and the fatherhood of God. Talking like that about other people goes against your own religious beliefs, and now you're talking about me and people I know and love."

The more difficult your own situation, the more important it is that you find support. Turn to your rabbi, your spouse, teachers, group leaders, and classmates in your conversion course, and other Jews-by-choice. Some converts have found it helpful to speak with their parents' clergyman, or a trusted friend of the family who can act both as a sympathetic sounding board for their feelings and as an advocate for you.[14] If there is a family breakdown, it may be useful to seek professional help to sort out the underlying family dynamics.

Since you are the person responsible for turning your family of origin into an interfaith family, it also becomes your responsibility to answer their questions about Judaism and

Jews. Don't wait for them to ask for information. Recommend or give them a few of the books and articles that you found useful; these can introduce them to some of the basic vocabulary of your Jewish life and provide a foundation for further discussion. Don't recommend any book you haven't read yourself, and don't limit reading suggestions to "Introduction to Judaism" literature. Sometimes, fiction or biography conveys information in more personal and compelling ways.

And don't expect books to teach your family everything they want or need to know. If your parents have never been inside a synagogue, invite them for a tour—perhaps accompanied by your rabbi. This is an especially good idea if you want your parents to attend a synagogue service honoring your conversion or if a Jewish wedding is in the offing.

Nevertheless, your parents may not be ready for a full immersion in Jewish life and culture. Some converts have unrealistic expectations of family members, who may be too overwhelmed or confused to comfortably attend your conversion service or to participate in a Jewish wedding ceremony. Respect their limits. And respect your own, too. Taking on a new religious identity is an enormous change, and your needs take precedence. As you grow more comfortable and confident as a Jew, you will become a better teacher and guide for your family.

Dayenu

When I die, my children will say
Kaddish for me and that, with pinewood box
and linen shroud, will be enough.

In time, I will say Kaddish
for my parents. It will not be enough.
They believe in Hell's Yellow Emperor,
fret about food, shelter for their ghosts.
The magnification of an alien God's name
would send them into the afterlife, barefoot
ghosts on hard dirt streets, banging
tin cups on red doors. They would drink
bitter tea, lie alongside ghosts with unopened wombs.

So I have promised my mother I will burn
a paper mansion with puppet servants, chests
of paper gold, paper shells of cars.
My brothers will provide oolong
and chicken rice each feast day, the monthly
stipend of Hell money, shells of faith.
These we render to our mother who tied
red thread on our feet and fingers as we slid
from her womb to bind us to life.

We hold this end of the scarlet thread
our parents unravel as they near the Yellow Springs,
feel it tighten as the wind
blowing off the river, lodges dust in our eyes.

HILARY THAM [15]

Honoring Your Children

*W*HEN PARENTS BECOME JEWS, what happens to their children?

Although a majority of conversions take place among young adults prior to marriage and/or parenthood, more people are choosing Judaism later in life and questions about converts' children arise with increasing frequency. Each case is unique. Some parents convert after many years of marriage, having lived a de facto Jewish life that included raising Jewish children. Others convert prior to a second marriage to a Jew, unsure about what they can fairly demand or expect of young children who believe in Santa Claus. Some children are delighted by the news of a parents' conversion, others mystified, still others fearful that this change represents some kind of abandonment. Some children are furious.

What you tell your children and how you respond to their concerns depends upon their ages and temperaments, as well as their previous religious education, affiliation, and identity. When there's been a divorce, the wishes of the other parent must be taken into account. In any event, children of all ages need reassurance that conversion to Judaism won't affect your love for them.

If you are thinking about formally converting a child, put aside your own wishes and listen without comment to what your son or daughter has to say about the idea. Discuss the matter with your rabbi, read the chapter called "Conversion of Children," and then do what you think is best for your child.

Whatever your situation, you are not the first person to

confront this dilemma. Find others who have been there before you. The teachers and social workers who lead conversion classes may be able to help put you in touch with other parents who converted. Counselors from your local Jewish family and children's services agency may be of assistance, too.

If you hope that your school-age children will ultimately choose to become Jews as well, consider these words of Rabbi Abraham Joshua Heschel:

> *I am a father. I have a daughter and I love her dearly. I would like my daughter to obey the commandments of the Torah; I would like her to revere me as her father. And so I ask myself the question over and over again: "What is there about me that deserves the reverence of my daughter?"*
>
> *You see, unless I live a life that is worthy of her reverence, I make it almost impossible for her to live a Jewish life. So many young people abandon Judaism because the Jewish models that they see in their parents are not worthy of reverence.*

Joining a Jewish Family

NINETY PERCENT of all converts to Judaism have a Jewish partner, which means that, for better and for worse, the vast majority of Jews-by-choice become part of an extended Jewish family.[16] Most Jewish spouses are enthusiastic partners in the process of conversion, some are ambivalent, and a few are downright hostile to the whole idea. Some Jewish families act as welcoming mentors to the new Jew, others are suspicious and cold. Whatever the situation, remember that your conversion may mark a new chapter in the life of your Jewish family as well as your family of origin and you may not be seeing them at their best.[17]

It may help you to know that in the past, conversion for the sake of marriage was suspect and even discouraged among Jews. The only conversions most rabbis considered acceptable were pure acts of faith—conversions "for the sake of heaven." Given that women have always comprised the vast majority of religious converts and that society usually grants greater economic and social power to men, a fiancée's or wife's conversion was commonly viewed not as an authentic religious choice but as acquiescence to a man's wishes or even as a way to achieve a better life.[18]

Old assumptions die hard. If you are dating, living with, engaged to, or married to a Jew, many people—including your partner's family and maybe even your partner—may think that you are converting *for* him or her, or *for* the marriage, or *for* your children. Actually, there's nothing wrong with those reasons *if*—and this is a crucial if—you are making the decision for yourself as well. A self-sacrificing conversion would be worse than a sham, it would be a sin.

But the fact is, many people find a spiritual home in Judaism as a result of falling in love with a Jew. As one Jew-by-choice wrote, "What better way to discover Judaism than through love? People sometimes say deprecatingly: 'Oh, she converted for marriage.' Or 'Oh, he converted for her.' . . . The point is: in these instances, the non-Jewish lover sees the beautiful in his beloved and identifies with it. What is it but the Jewishness of the Jew that he wants? And so he chooses to become a Jew himself. This is not something to scoff at. Judaism can be discerned in the beauty of its people, in their love."[19]

The sincerity and commitment of converts who come to Judaism through romantic love has been demonstrated so often and in so many settings, the long-standing rejection of prospective converts who are dating or engaged to born-Jews has started to fade—even among the most traditional elements of the Jewish world.[20] Rabbi Joseph B. Soloveichik, one of the great teachers of modern Orthodoxy, wrote:

> *We don't have the strength to convince a young man or woman who has fallen in love with a non-Jew [not to marry them]. There is no formula—not even the best Jewish education—which is able to function as a shield in the face of this phenomenon. After the fact, the possibility of dissuasion is very weak. . . . The correct way is specifically the way of the Reform (and I am sure many of my Orthodox friends will stone me on account of what I am saying)—of course with Orthodox content. . . . We must develop programs and methods to integrate them under the wings of God's presence and to make them good Jews. . . . There are Jews whose wives, born gentiles, have brought their [Jewish] husbands back to Judaism.[21]*

Your Jewish Partner

ACCORDING TO THE MIDRASH, God creates new worlds constantly by causing marriages to take place. If Judaism and Jewishness didn't matter to your Jewish partner, you probably wouldn't be reading this book. So, whether or not he or she can explain why, your spouse probably wants the "new world" you create together to have a Jewish atmosphere, a Jewish address.

Some Jewish spouses can articulate why they hope you will convert. They may tell you it's because being Jewish is an integral part of who they are, or because Judaism gives meaning and shape to their lives, and because they want to share these things with you and your children. But other Jews who have not set foot inside a synagogue for years may weep at the idea of having a priest officiate at their wedding—without being able to explain why. For some born-Jews, their fiancé's conversion class is the first formal Jewish education they ever received. For others, conversion classes are a way to reconnect with something set aside long ago. You'll hear these kinds of stories and many more during the group discussion sessions that are part of nearly all conversion classes.

Whatever your partner's background, it's important to start talking about what Judaism means to each of you early in the conversion process—and to keep on talking as you progress down this road. The main reason why rabbis insist that both partners attend conversion classes and meetings is to ensure that you have this discussion. The conversations you share on the way home from your classes and meetings may be the most important part of the conversion process.

It's not unusual for couples to discover that they have different religious interests and styles. Virtually all couples—including those who come from the same background—have to negotiate and compromise around religious matters, and it's common for one member of a couple to be more "into it" than the other. Sometimes, converts become more interested in Jewish observance than their born-Jewish spouses. Over time, interests ebb and flow, and at some point you may even switch roles. Mutual respect is essential in navigating these waters.

This isn't to suggest that you should ignore serious disagreements. If you discover, for instance, that your spouse sees the *mikvah* as the end of all the Jewish "stuff" while you view it as just the beginning, or if prayer is deeply meaningful to you and an object of disdain for him/her, you may face major problems later on. Your rabbi may be able to facilitate a conversation about such issues or he/she can point you to a spiritually sensitive therapist. The Reform movement offers a variety of groups, classes, and workshops with such names as "New Beginnings: Yours, Mine, and Ours," and "Times and Seasons," where intermarried couples explore differences in a safe, supportive environment. The Jewish Board of Family and Children's Services agency in your community may run groups or offer couples counseling. The Jewish Converts Network sponsors groups for intermarried couples as well.

Rabbis and therapists agree, however, that serious and protracted arguments focused on religious differences are usually not about religion at all, but point to more fundamental issues in a relationship.

And some differences are inevitable. After all, you got to choose Judaism, while your partner may feel it was thrust upon her. You may feel jealous and bereft because you have no childhood memories of Jewish holidays to look back upon, while he may envy your freedom from deadly dull afternoons in Hebrew classes.

On the other hand, your spouse may not be sensitive to the limits of being a Jew-by-choice. After all, your siblings probably won't be sitting *shiva* with you after a parent dies, and it may take many years before you feel you really belong in temple. You may find yourself envying your own children's early Jewish memories.

Of course, the differences between you and your spouse probably have something to do with why you were attracted to each other in the first place. Some psychologists claim that Jews choose non-Jewish spouses, at least in part, to escape from their Jewishness or from an overly intense or "hot" family dynamics they perceive as essentially Jewish.[22] By the same token, some Jews are drawn to the "cooler," less enmeshed, and more independent personality of non-Jews.[23] Even so, people fall in love and marry for complicated and mysterious reasons, and it would be a mistake to lay too much at the door of ethnic or religious difference.

Your In-laws and the Rest of the Mishpachah*

THERE'S AN OLD JOKE:

A Jewish boy is about to leave for college when his father takes him aside and says, "Look, we've never been a religious family, but please, promise that you won't go and marry a *shiksa*."† The son promises.

During his senior year, however, he falls in love with a non-Jewish woman. After serious thought and study, she converts and they marry. The couple moves back to the son's hometown and he goes to work in his father's business.

A few weeks after the couple has gotten settled, the phone rings in their home. The father is on the line, asking his son, "Where are you? We always go over the books on the last Saturday of the month."

The son says, "I can't come. My wife says it's forbidden to work on Shabbat." To which the father replies, "I told you not to marry a *shiksa*."[24]

Sometimes, you just can't win. Like when one young man told his Jewish in-laws that he had decided to convert and their immediate response was, "Your poor parents!"

In general, conversion tends to ease relationships with Jewish families, which view intermarriage with dismay, and any resistance to your marriage will probably crumble as ten-

---

* mishpachah—*Yiddish and Hebrew for family*
† shiksa—*used to denote a female gentile*

sions over the identity of future grandchildren are erased. If your conversion follows years of marriage to a Jew, the rest of the family may be overjoyed and throw you a big party. Then again, your choice may utterly baffle them and leave them unsure about how to react to you.

Regardless of the circumstances of your conversion, your Jewish family's response will depend not only on your relationship to them but also on their own Jewish identity. If you are the first convert in the family, it's likely that you will be a magnet for curiosity, questions, and comments that may seem extraordinarily rude.

Probably the most common offense against converts, usually committed without any malice, is the use of the words *shiksa* and *shaygetz*. As in, "Here is Miriam's husband, Matt, who used to be a *shaygetz* but converted." Or, "This is my beautiful *shiksa* daughter-in-law, who is a better Jew than me!"

Most Jews think that *shiksa* means "female gentile" and *shaygetz* "male gentile," but in fact, those words are anything but neutral. They mean "abomination" and convey the fact that non-Jews were strictly forbidden as marriage partners. While the offense is unintended, these words unconsciously reflect the belief that Jewishness is an ontological category—a status you're either born with or not. More than a few Jews-by-choice have been hurt by the announcement "I don't believe in conversion. A person can't just *become* Jewish."

While the use of words like *shiksa* and the idea of an inborn Jewishness are rarely meant as insults to anyone in particular, Jews are not exempt from bigotry. Just as some non-Jews still believe that all Jews are stingy, some Jews harbor stereotypes about non-Jewish stupidity. It's painful to find those attitudes among your extended family, but there's no reason to let bigoted comments go unchallenged: "Oh, Al, I can't believe you said that. My parents are non-Jews and you know they're intelligent and hardworking people."

Whether or not it's always a welcome role, converts often end up as teachers and role models for Jews as well as for non-Jews. Your presence complicates and disturbs a sense of reality grounded in a very different period of history—when Jews were Jews no matter what they didn't do, and when gentiles could never become Jews, no matter what they did. If you—with your blond hair, or your black skin, or your Asian eyes—are a more knowledgeable, observant, and committed Jew than they are, then what does it mean to be a Jew in name only? Few people welcome such a serious challenge to their world view.

Within your Jewish family, you and your partner may be the first Jews in a generation to light Shabbat candles or join a synagogue. While this may delight some of your relatives, it may cause discomfort, embarrassment, shame, or misplaced anger among others. Most Jews-by-choice try to minimize contact with the naysayers in their families and seek out allies. But you can also open long-closed doors within your extended Jewish family; sometimes all it takes is a few questions. Ask your in-laws, or your wife's aunt, where the family name comes from. From which cities or *shtetl*s in Europe did the family emigrate? Who was Grandpa Max named after? What does Grandma remember about her childhood Hanukkah celebrations? The information unearthed as a result of your questions can knit a family together—with you as an integral part of the emerging pattern.

Not all Jewish families react coolly to converts. Many families take the Jew-by-choice under their wing, opening homes and hearts, sharing traditions and recipes, handing down heirlooms. One woman says that her conversion took place not only in the *mikvah* but also in the kitchen, where her Jewish mother-in-law and Jewish grandmother-in-law taught her how to make favorite family meals and welcomed her into the world of Jewish women.

Of course, there can be too much of a good thing, as when family members presume to tell you how to live your Jewish life. Your father-in-law may be horrified by your child-centered seder that substitutes a puppet show for pages and pages of the text he's heard since boyhood. Your sister-in-law might inform you that membership in a Reform temple is tantamount to joining an Episcopal church. Then again, you might scandalize your relatives by refusing to miss Shabbat dinner and attend basketball games on Friday nights with the rest of the family.

As you establish your own Jewish home, and especially as you explore Jewish life through the eyes of your children, you will create traditions of your own. And your branch of the family tree will have an independent life, connected yet distinct.

Homecoming: If One of Your Parents (or Grandparents) Is Jewish

*I*N HIS MEMOIR, *Lovesong: Becoming a Jew*, Julius Lester attributes his lifelong attraction to Jewish music, worship, and prayer to an innate yearning he inherited from a man he never met—his maternal great-grandfather, who was a Jew. Lester's strong, almost mystical connection to Judaism is not uncommon among converts. Many Jews-by-choice discover a Jewish ancestor in their family tree in the process of converting. Adoptees have learned that one or both of their birth parents or biological grandparents were Jewish.

Some of these stories are quite remarkable. When a young Puerto Rican man told his Catholic mother he had decided to convert to Judaism, she became furious and shouted, "I thought all of that ended with your grandmother!" Her words recalled how the young man's grandmother used to go to the basement on Friday nights to light candles; apparently she was a *conversa*, the offspring of Jews who publicly converted in order to escape the persecutions of the Inquisition in fifteenth-century Spain and Portugal, but continued to practice Jewish rituals in secret.

The Jewish mystical tradition explains this phenomenon with the legend of the *gilgul*. According to the fourteenth-century text *Sefer ha pliya* (The Book of Marvels),[25] a *gilgul* is a Jewish soul that was somehow lost or separated from Judaism. The means of separation vary and are of secondary importance: Once there was a Jewish orphan who was adopted by gentile parents. . . . Once there was a Jew who converted to Christianity. . . . However the story begins, the Jewish soul passes from one generation to the next, living a Christian or Muslim life. But eventually the soul's yearning for Jewish expression grows overwhelming, seeks out other Jews, and finds its way "home."

Of course, many converts who have no Jewish ancestry at all also describe a feeling of homecoming when they discover and embrace Judaism, and there is a danger in placing too much emphasis on a biological or mystical explanation for why people convert. Judaism is an attractive, rich, satisfying tradition, and Jews-by-choice enter the house of Israel through many doors and for many reasons.

The process of conversion is always the same, regardless of Jewish ancestry. The preparation and study, the rituals, ceremonies, and celebrations for conversion are the same for everyone. Nonetheless, reconnecting to a lost or forgotten heritage has its own emotional resonance. The choice of a Hebrew name can give you the opportunity to reach back to generations past, and certainly the story of your Jewish journey is a treasure to share and to study. Genealogical research is a popular avocation in the Jewish community, and there are many resources to help you learn more about the Jewish roots and branches of your family tree.

But sometimes, the connection to Judaism is very clear. Myra, for example, was raised as a Jew and given a religious school education. She married a Jew, belonged to a synagogue, and was thinking about sending her children to a Jewish day school when the school's headmaster told Myra that before her children would be permitted to enroll, she and her sons would have to convert.

"Convert?" she asked, in some distress. "From what?"

The issue—for the headmaster—was the fact that Myra's mother had never formally converted, which meant that Jewish law did not recognize her or her children as Jews.

Myra decided to explore conversion as a way to spare her children a similar challenge to their identity later in life and found a sensitive rabbi who helped her identify her particular situation as a "halachic dilemma"—a problem based solely in traditional Jewish law, which is unyielding on this point. He told Myra that "conversion" was probably the wrong term for her situation, and suggested that she think of the *mikvah* as a formal affirmation of her family's Jewishness.

Technically, the "affirmation" was a conversion, complete with a *mikvah* witnessed by a *bet din*. Myra and her children went to the *mikvah,* where they recited the traditional Hebrew blessings for immersion.[26] (Since her sons had undergone *brit milah* by a *mohel* as infants, the rabbis decided there was no need for the ritual of *hatafat dam brit*.) Following the trip to the *mikvah,* Myra threw a "Jewish birthday party" for her family.

Says Myra, "Of course, Orthodox Jews might still not recognize me as a Jew, but at least I feel I've done what I need to do to be 'kosher' in the parts of the Jewish community where I'm likely to have contact and that matter to me."

As a liberal Jew, Myra had the choice of simply ignoring any challenge to her authenticity. Reform and Reconstructionist rabbis would recognize Myra and her children as Jews.

In 1983, the Central Conference of American Rabbis, the rabbinical association of Reform rabbis, ruled that Reform Jews would recognize the Jewishness of any child if *either* parent was Jewish and the child was actively raised and educated as a Jew; conversion was deemed unnecessary. This decision, referred to as "patrilineal descent," was taken with the knowledge that Orthodox and Conservative Jews would not accept this step. Thus, Myra's case is not rare.

Many Jewish-identified offspring of intermarriages feel insecure about their status as Jews—and not only because of challenges from other people. For those who wish to affirm their Jewishness in a traditional manner, the notion of conversion-as-affirmation can be very helpful. "I know that some Jews might not recognize me or my children as Jewish—even after this," says Myra. "But I feel secure in a way I never did. And the experience itself was fabulous, meaningful, and even fun."

PART II

Preparation

*W*HAT SHOULD I READ?

*H*OW CAN I EVER LEARN ENOUGH?

*H*OW DO I FIND A RABBI TO TEACH ME?

*C*AN I BE JEWISH WITHOUT KNOWING HEBREW?

*H*OW DO I FIND A HEBREW NAME?

*H*OW DO I KNOW WHEN I'M READY?

*W*HY DO I HAVE TO CONVERT IF MY FATHER IS JEWISH?

$\mathcal{S}$OME PEOPLE CAN DATE THEIR ATTRACTION TO Judaism from a childhood experience. For many, falling in love with a Jew was the entry point. Others began the journey in a college philosophy class, or through conversations with Jewish co-workers and friends. Whatever the threshold, the "first step" in the process of converting to Judaism is almost never enrolling in a class or scheduling a meeting with a rabbi. And yet, once you make the decision to become a Jew, the path is remarkably consistent. Before you can undergo the rituals required of converts and before you will be accepted as a Jew by the community, you will be asked to do three things.

The first is to find a teacher—a rabbi—who will act as your guide and sponsor through the formal process of conversion.

The second is to begin—or further—your study of Judaism. Although no one is expected to become an expert or a scholar, becoming a Jew does require that you become a student of Judaism.

The third expectation is that you will begin to experience Judaism as a way of life. This means becoming aware of the Jewish calendar as much as possible—attending Sabbath services and celebrating Jewish holidays—and starting to explore the diversity of the Jewish community in search of your own place in it.

Choosing
Your Rabbi

Once, there was a disciple who left home to study with
a great and holy rabbi. When he returned to his village,
his friends gathered around to ask him about the ideas
and principles the great teacher had imparted.
But the disciple replied, "I went to the rabbi to learn
how he ties his shoelaces."

HASIDIC STORY

AT MOST JEWISH LIFE-CYCLE EVENTS, THE rabbi is optional. From a halachic or legal standpoint, a wedding, *bris,* bar or bat mitzvah, or funeral can be perfectly "kosher" in the absence of a rabbi. Conversion, however, requires the participation of a rabbi for the simple reason that becoming a Jew is largely a matter of study and the word "rabbi" means teacher.

Historically, becoming a Jew consisted solely of private study with an individual rabbi, who would then arrange the formal rituals of conversion, which included the convening of a *bet din,* a court of three rabbis. Among Orthodox Jews, private conversion is still the only option, and this remains a possibility for liberal conversion as well. However, given the numbers of candidates for conversion, the Conservative, Reconstructionist, and Reform movements run classes for prospective converts. Nevertheless, all movements still require a sponsoring or referring rabbi.

This rabbi is not merely a gatekeeper. The relationship between a Jew-by-choice and his or her rabbi is typically more intimate and complex than the kind of student-teacher exchange that takes place in a classroom. With some effort on your part—and a little luck—the rabbi who helps you become a Jew will become *your* rabbi.

To call someone "*my* rabbi" suggests a personal relationship based not only on an exchange of information. *Your* rabbi gets to know a good deal about you: your family of origin, your reasons for exploring Judaism, your doubts, and your dreams. *Your* rabbi is a person with whom you've discussed God and faith, community and commitment. *Your* rabbi has the right to ask you difficult questions during the course of your meetings together, and the obligation to address your difficult questions. *Your* rabbi is someone who inspires in you a love of Judaism, treats you like a *mensch* (a human being), and earns your respect.

People can and do convert to Judaism without making a deep, personal connection with a rabbi. And it's not fair—either to you or to your rabbi—to expect one person to be your only Jewish teacher. Although *your* rabbi might be the one who teaches you Hebrew and about the Holocaust and the holiday cycle, you can learn about those and other subjects in classes taught by other people and/or through independent reading. Indeed, since Judaism is pluralistic, democratic, and even contradictory, the more numerous your teachers, the better. Nevertheless, finding a good match (in Yiddish, a *shidduch*) with a rabbi can make the difference between an inspiring conversion experience and a disappointing one.

As in any profession, the rabbinate has its specialists and its generalists, its masters and its journeymen. Some rabbis are great preachers and teachers, others are superb listeners and pastoral counselors. Not everyone needs or wants a rabbi to be a spiritual guide. Not everyone needs or wants a rabbi to be a great scholar. However, everyone needs and has the right to expect his or her rabbi to be a *mensch*. It's pointless to try to learn Judaism from someone you don't like or respect, so trust your instincts and shop around.

HOW TO FIND *YOUR* RABBI: Given the personal nature of the convert-rabbi relationship, there is no one-size-fits-all formula for selecting a rabbi. However, with some basic information and a few strategies in hand, you should have an easier time finding a teacher who suits you.

Some people begin the conversion process already knowing their rabbi. You or your spouse might already belong to a congregation, or your fiancé may be affiliated with a synagogue. However, since a majority of converts to Judaism are not connected with a congregation or rabbi, finding the right person often requires some legwork.

Word-of-mouth referrals are the best place to start. Ask Jews you know if they're affiliated with a congregation and then ask whether—and why—they like their rabbi. If you like what you hear, you can simply pick up the phone and ask for an appointment.

Most non-Orthodox rabbis are willing to teach converts; however, their abilities and interests do vary.[1] Some are inspiring and devoted mentors who accept as many students as they can fit into their schedules. Other rabbis are not so inclined, or are simply too busy to devote the amount of time it takes to do justice to a serious newcomer to Judaism. Since many prospective converts are not synagogue members, teaching them also takes time away from other congregational duties. Of course, if you are already a member of a rabbi's synagogue, or if you are married or engaged to a member, your needs are very much his or her concern, and in all likelihood, he or she will try to accommodate you.

If you are associated with a university, the campus Hillel[2] rabbi is a logical place to start since you are, in effect, a part of his or her congregation. However, it's important to remember that Hillel rabbis, like all American rabbis, run the gamut in terms of affiliation and interest. If the campus rabbi is not welcoming or is too busy to help you, don't give up. He or she should be able to give you the names of other rabbis in the community.

If you don't have a local contact and want to talk to a Reform rabbi, call Reform Jewish Outreach at the Union of American Hebrew Congregations (UAHC),* which can either

---

* See Resources for a list of names, addresses, and telephone numbers of national organizations mentioned in this section.

put you in touch with the regional office or send you a list of the Reform rabbis in your community. Regional offices of the UAHC run Outreach programs and offer "Introduction to Judaism" courses, which are taught by local rabbis. (Outreach classes are also a good way to check out rabbis, who teach the courses.) Local Outreach directors or coordinators can be an excellent source of referrals, since they are familiar with area Reform rabbis—and often Conservative rabbis, too.

To find a Conservative rabbi, a local chapter of the United Synagogue of Conservative Judaism should be able to provide you with a list of names and information about Conservative conversion programs. The Rabbinical Assembly in New York City can also provide the names of area synagogues and rabbis.

To find a Reconstructionist rabbi, call the Jewish Reconstructionist Federation for names and numbers.

Once you've identified a likely candidate, try to attend a service at her synagogue. If you liked what she had to say and if you were impressed by "how she ties her shoes," approach her at the social hour that typically follows the service (called an *oneg Shabbat* on Friday night, or the *kiddush* on Saturday morning), introduce yourself, and explain that you're interested in converting to Judaism and would like to make an appointment to discuss studying with her.

If you're too shy or just don't get the opportunity to make contact after the service, your follow-up phone call should include mention of the fact that you recently attended services at her congregation. Your presence at synagogue indicates that you're a serious student and should get you an appointment with even the busiest rabbi.

Some converts face pressure from their Jewish partners or from prospective in-laws to study with a particular rabbi or to convert through the auspices of their movement. This can become a point of contention, especially if you can't see yourself working with your in-laws' rabbi, or if *your* rabbi is not affiliated with the denomination your partner prefers. As a student of Judaism, try to remain open to all of the possibilities; remember that the decision concerning where to begin the process of conversion does not obligate you to finish there. Nevertheless, this is a crucial choice and it is yours to make. Once you've done some research, discussed the options with your partner, and selected a teacher who is right for you, your decision should be honored.

YOUR FIRST MEETING: Many rabbis, when asked for an initial appointment to discuss conversion, will ask you to bring your Jewish partner (if you have one). Since couples are sometimes wrestling with religious conflicts, the rabbi may want to get those out on the table right away. However, if you'd rather go alone, make your preference known.

You can expect to be nervous, anxious, or even guilty about your first meeting. Even if you've known the rabbi for years, this appointment marks the beginning of a different kind of relationship.

Be prepared to answer questions—some specific, but mostly general and open-ended. There are no trick questions and no trapdoors. You will not be asked whether you believe in God, or to repudiate your family, or to make any promises at all. The rabbi will simply ask you to talk about yourself, your work, your childhood, your parents. He will probably ask why you're thinking about conversion at this point in your life, whether your family is aware of your interest in Judaism, and if so, what they think of it. You may be asked to talk about your religious upbringing, and whether you are currently a member of a church.

Be honest and don't worry about judgments. This is simply an "intake interview," and there aren't any right or wrong answers. It's highly unlikely that you'll be asked about anything that you haven't already considered.

The rabbi may want to determine whether you're converting for your own reasons rather than for your fiancé's, or your husband's, or your in-laws'. If you are still attending church, most rabbis will ask whether you've talked with your minister or priest. If you haven't told your parents about your decision to convert, the rabbi might suggest that you talk to them before meeting with him again.

Do come prepared with questions of your own. You might even want to write them down in the likely event of nervous amnesia. By the end of your first meeting, you should know what the rabbi requires in the way of formal and/or informal study, how long the conversion process usually takes, and his ritual requirements.

Some Reform and Reconstructionist rabbis offer *mikvah, hatafat dam brit,* and *bet din* as "options" available to the convert, but others require all of the above. Conservative rabbis require all of the traditional ritual elements, plus a promise to "observe the *mitzvot.*" Many liberal rabbis also offer or urge a public conversion ceremony of welcome.

By the end of your first meeting, you and the rabbi may agree to begin studying. Or he may ask you to think about it and call back with a decision. On reflection, consider whether you felt comfortable with the rabbi. Imagine what it might be like to ask this person tough questions, such as "What if I don't believe in God?" or "Am I ever going to feel Jewish?" If you can't imagine being honest and at ease with this person, make an appointment with someone else. Choosing a rabbi is an important decision, so take your time.

YOUR RABBI, YOUR SPOUSE, AND YOU: Since most conversions involve a born-Jewish partner, many rabbis require that your fiancé or spouse participate in all classes and meetings—or at least most of them. Attending meetings with the rabbi can be a wonderful experience for a couple, giving you the opportunity to talk about serious matters you might never otherwise discuss. One rabbi tells his students for conversion, "Actually, the time you two spend in the car coming to and going home from our meetings is probably the most important part of this whole process."

The choice of a rabbi can become a flash point for couples, however, especially if the born-Jewish partner is alienated from Judaism. Many Jews who have distanced themselves from synagogue life retain negative childhood images of "the Rabbi," and may be intimidated by, suspicious of, or even downright hostile to anyone who bears the title. These kinds of attitudes can be confusing to the convert and may even undermine your relationship to the rabbi. The issue may not be the rabbi at all, but an expression of the born-Jew's ambivalence about his or her Judaism. This is the kind of problem that may be addressed during the group discussions led by social workers or psychologists, which are part of virtually all formal conversion courses.

STUDYING WITH YOUR RABBI: At your first meeting, the rabbi should outline his or her study requirements and expectations. Generally, you will be asked to meet on a regular basis (from biweekly to monthly) over a period of time ranging from six months to two years; the average is about one year. These sessions are usually held in the rabbi's office.

Your meetings will focus on books the rabbi asks you to buy and read. These books, which will become part of your Jewish home library, are intended to provide an introduction to a variety of subjects and concepts. Although specific titles vary, you can expect to read about Sabbath and holiday observance, the Jewish life cycle, Jewish history, the Holocaust, the state of Israel, theology, and spirituality. The assignments are geared to stimulate questions and conversations.

In addition to reading, some rabbis require (and others suggest) that you keep a journal during the conversion process. In some cases, the rabbi will ask to read what you've written. But most often, your journal will remain a private diary for collecting thoughts and perhaps jotting down questions to bring up during meetings. In any case, such a record can become a precious document of a very powerful period of transition in your life.

As the time of your formal conversion approaches, some rabbis ask that you write a paper on a topic of your choosing, or compose a personal statement about why you are becoming a Jew.

Judaism is a highly literary tradition. However, not all Jews are scholars or academics or even great readers. Tell your rabbi if your learning style is better served in some other fashion. And because there is much more to Judaism than reading and writing, most rabbis also assign hands-on "lessons." You will probably be asked to attend worship services regularly, and perhaps to go to synagogues of various denominations in order to experience Judaism's religious diversity. You may also be encouraged to experiment with Sabbath observance, to go shopping at a kosher butcher shop, to attend a concert of Jewish music. Some rabbis will ask whether you would like a Jewish mentor, a layperson who will include you in family Shabbat and holiday observances and be available to answer any questions you might not feel comfortable asking the rabbi.

At any point in your conversion studies, you are free to stop. You may decide, even after several months, that the rabbi you started out with is not the right teacher for you. Or you may simply need to take a break. Never forget that this is a journey of your own choosing and of your own design.

Indeed, the more you can become a partner in the process of your own conversion, the more you'll get from the experience. Even the best-intentioned rabbi can only guess at your needs and interests, so it is essential that you make yourself clear. Given the enormous breadth and depth of the Jewish library—from fiction to mysticism to medical ethics—there are countless ways for individuals to connect with the tradition. So if you are intrigued by some area of Jewish thought or culture that the rabbi either didn't cover or only mentioned in passing, ask if you can discuss it further, or at least request suggestions for additional reading. Your initiative and interest will inspire your rabbi and enrich your relationship.

CANTORS: Although it is not common, some people pursue their studies with cantors rather than rabbis—usually because they've made a strong personal connection with a willing cantor.

A cantor is a person trained in Jewish liturgical music who leads synagogue services. In the past, cantors were liturgists, people who knew the melodies for the various holidays and religious services. Today, however, the role of the cantor (in Hebrew *chazzan, chazzanit* for a woman) has changed dramatically. Cantors who are "vested" (the cantorial version of ordination) by the Reform and Conservative movements receive at least four years of seminary training, which includes courses in Jewish history and law, and pastoral relationships.

Cantors function as clergy, and in many synagogues they do a great deal of teaching to children, bar and bat mitzvah students, and adults. In most states, they are licensed to perform weddings, and cantors routinely officiate at funerals and at ceremonies for new babies. Cantors often serve on non-Orthodox *bet din*s for conversion.

PAYMENT: Although you should expect to pay for organized conversion classes, for books, and for the costs associated with the *mikvah* and/or ritual circumcision, it is generally not considered appropriate to pay a congregational rabbi (or cantor) for his or her part in the conversion process. Aiding a sincere convert is considered a *mitzvah*—a good and holy act—done for its own sake.

However, it is a lovely gesture for a Jew-by-choice to make a gift of *tzedakah* (charity) in the rabbi's honor upon the occasion of his or her conversion. Such a donation honors the rabbi in two ways: in addition to being an expression of thanks and respect, it also demonstrates your understanding of this primary Jewish obligation. Gifts may be made to the rabbi's discretionary fund or to any Jewish charitable organization.

If you and the rabbi have developed a close relationship, you might want to give a personal gift as well, such as a Jewish work of art, a recording of Jewish music, or perhaps a gift certificate to a bookstore. But a personal letter from you to your rabbi expressing your thoughts about the path you've followed together to this point is probably the best gift you can give.

March 9, 1991
Rabbi David Wolfman
Temple Isaiah
Lexington, Mass.

Dear Rabbi Wolfman:
Probably to you the thirteenth of March comes and goes like any other day — but not so for me. For me the thirteenth of March marks a very important moment in my life — the one-year anniversary of the day I chose Judaism.
I have to admit that in the days and weeks immedi-

ately following the mikvah *and conversion ceremony, I didn't have much of a reaction. At first, I was numb and so busy trying to decide how I felt that I felt nothing. And then came the wedding, which took up time and emotional energy. But slowly, after everything had calmed down, it began to sink in. . . . The day I told my hairdresser without a pause, "Oh, we're Jewish," when she asked me what church Dan and I went to. The Friday night when I scrambled in cabinets and drawers all over the house because we were out of candles and it just wouldn't be Shabbat without them. The day I cried because I missed Christmas and felt guilty for feeling that way. The day a friend called me on the phone to ask about a Jewish wedding custom and I was able to answer her! Lots of little moments like these helped me start to fit into this new part of myself.*

Some of the experiences weren't so little. Like Yom Kippur, when I needed to be with my sick grandmother. I sat in her rural Pennsylvania home and read aloud from the Yom Kippur service all by myself, wishing I could be at temple. And, of course, the war, when I sometimes felt I didn't have as much right as a "real Jew" to be horrified and concerned at the involvement of Israel in the conflict and to give opinions about the Arab-Israeli situation. The night that Israel was attacked, I was in a restaurant with two girlfriends. When the waiter told us what had happened, one of them said lightly, "Well, at least none of us here is Jewish." And although I corrected her, I felt odd and went home right way to watch CNN and to be with Dan.

I guess for me this process of "feeling Jewish" is an on-

going one. *Once in a while, I still feel like I'm in limbo—what is my real identity? But most of the time, I don't even think about it. I just am what I am. Choosing Judaism has not made me a different person altogether, but it has profoundly affected many parts of me. In the past few years since joining Temple Isaiah, my life has been enriched immeasurably, and I only hope that I can offer to Judaism as much as I have received.*

I know it's not customary to discuss the conversion once the process is complete, and I assure you that usually I am rather circumspect. No, I can't say that I shout it from the rooftops, but I can't deny that nearly every day I shout it from my soul.

Jeanne Lovy

Study

*Holy One of Blessing, Your Presence Fills Creation, You
make us holy with Your commandments and call us to
occupy ourselves with words of Torah.*

BLESSING RECITED BEFORE JEWISH STUDY

IF YOU ARE IN THE PROCESS OF BECOMING A
Jew, clear off a bookshelf. Better yet, buy a new bookcase.

Your sponsoring rabbi will doubtless ask you to buy several books in the course of your studies together. If you are also enrolled in a conversion class, you'll be assigned at least a few more. If these volumes are your first Jewish books, they will constitute the foundation of your own Jewish home library, which means you're on your way to creating a Jewish home.

The prospect of trying to "learn" Judaism—a religious civilization with four thousand years of history and millions of book titles—is overwhelming. But the goal of the reading you'll be asked to do is not to make you an expert or a scholar. Your conversion studies are intended only to give you an overview, and an appreciation. The famous Talmudic story about Hillel, one of the greatest Jewish teachers of all time, applies to you:

A man went looking for Rabbi Hillel and said to him, "I want to become a Jew. But only on the condition that you teach me the Torah, all of it, while I stand on one foot." Hillel looked at this smart-aleck and said, "What is hateful to you, do not do to your fellow man. That is the entire Torah—all of it. The rest is commentary. Go and study."

The last line is the key. "Go and study" is your homework assignment.

But doing this homework is not really a means to an end. Jewish study is a *mitzvah*—a sacred obligation or righteous deed. Indeed, Torah study is traditionally considered the essential and ultimate *mitzvah*. In the words of the Talmud:

> These are the obligations without measure,
> whose reward, too, is without measure:
> To honor mother and father,
> to perform acts of loving-kindness,
> to attend the house of study daily,
> to welcome the stranger,
> to visit the sick,
> to rejoice with the bride and bridegroom,
> to comfort the bereaved,
> to pray with sincerity,
> to make peace when there is strife.
> And the study of Torah is equal to them all
> because the study of Torah leads to them all.[3]

STUDY AS SPIRITUAL PRACTICE: When a Jewish baby is born, and again when he or she reaches the age of bar or bat mitzvah, parents and friends pray, "May he [or she] grow up to a life of Torah, *huppah,* and *ma'asim tovim.*"[4]

Huppah refers to the marriage canopy—to human love and a commitment to family. *Ma'asim tovim* means "good deeds"—working to make the world a better place. But the first item on this short list is always Torah—the study of Torah.

Torah is a complicated word. "The Torah" refers to the first five books of the Hebrew Bible, which are also called the Pentateuch or the five books of Moses. A Torah is the hand-written scroll from which Jews read in an annual cycle from Genesis, Exodus, Leviticus, Numbers, and Deuteronomy. "Torah" can also be used to refer to the entire Hebrew Bible,* to all Jewish commentary on the Bible, to the entire library of Jewish thought, and even to the idea of revelation itself.[5] "Torah study," however, refers to the serious yet lively reading and rereading of the first five books of the Bible.

When your formal studies for conversion come to an end, your "life of Torah" begins. According to tradition, Jewish peoplehood began at Mount Sinai when God gave the Torah to Israel as a source of blessing and life. In other words,[6]

---

* *The word "Bible" comes from the Latin* biblia, *meaning "books." When Jews talk about the Bible, they are referring to the Jewish or Hebrew Bible, which is what Christians call the "Old Testament." According to Christian belief, Jesus announced a new covenant between God and humankind, which was spelled out in the "New Testament." The Hebrew name for the Bible is Tanach, an acronym that refers to the three kinds of books of which it is comprised: T—Torah, N—Nivi'im, or Prophets, and CH—Ketubim, or Writings.*

God gave the Jews the Torah and said, "Here. Take this book home and tell Me what you think about it." And ever since, Jews have been telling God—and each other—what they think God's book is all about. These commentaries appear in the Talmud and in rabbis' sermons, in works of fiction and nonfiction, and especially in conversation whenever two or more Jews study Torah together.

The uniquely Jewish approach to Torah study is through a process called *midrash.* From the Hebrew word for "seek," "search," or even "demand,"[7] *midrash* transforms reading into an imaginative yet disciplined search for revelation, typified by a passion that is simultaneously personal and collective, academic and creative, hard work and great fun.

Perhaps one reason why Judaism locates its spiritual center in the Torah is because its study is so firmly grounded in human relationships. Solitary study is explicitly discouraged in the Talmud, which counsels, "Get yourself a teacher and find yourself a fellow student," and "Form groups for the purpose of study, for Torah can be acquired only in a group." Perhaps the real secret of Jewish survival is the thirty-five-hundred-year-old conversation that goes on in those groups.

That conversation has always been a knock-down, drag-out debate. Converts seeking a catechism of faith to memorize are often confused and disappointed by Jewish pedagogy, which is dialectical and argumentative. Becoming a Jew means learning to plunge into the give-and-take of Talmudic argument. Indeed, argument is preserved (if not sanctified) in the Talmud, which retains minority opinions that were overruled centuries ago!

The intellectual challenge embedded in Jewish study is one reason people have been drawn to Judaism throughout the ages. When you become a Jew, you have not only the right but also a responsibility to join the debate. You'll have reached a milestone in your Jewish journey the day you hear yourself publicly disagree about the meaning of a Jewish text (or sermon, or ritual) with your rabbi (or Jewish spouse or in-laws).

CONVERSION CLASSES: Most rabbis require that prospective converts enroll in an introductory class offered by one of the three liberal movements (see Resources). These courses include lectures, reading assignments, and small group discussions facilitated by social workers. Sessions last anywhere from six to eight months.

The lectures are generally a mixed bag and range in quality from inspirational to dull, but the course as a whole always provides important experiences for prospective Jews. For one thing, they are usually taught by a team of rabbis, which gives you a chance to experience a variety of rabbinical approaches and styles. And the fact that these courses tend to be large should reassure you that you are not alone in this journey; indeed, you may make some very good friends in class.

Generally, the formal homework consists of assigned reading, and some teachers ask that you keep a reading journal. Some conversion courses also require a research paper on an approved topic of your own choosing, and/or a take-home exam.

No two courses feature exactly the same syllabus, but over the course of the class you can expect to hear lectures, participate in discussions, and read about the following topics:

- SHABBAT AND THE HOLIDAYS: The meaning and rituals of the Sabbath; observing the annual holiday cycle, usually beginning with the Holy Days of Rosh Hashanah and Yom Kippur

- THE JEWISH LIFE CYCLE: Customs and rituals for birth, bar and bat mitzvah, weddings, funerals (and sometimes adoption and conversion, too)

- LIVING A JEWISH LIFE: Creating a Jewish home, connecting with the Jewish community

- HISTORY: An overview of four thousand years, including biblical times, the Rabbinic period, the Middle Ages, the Enlightenment, Emancipation, and the American Jewish experience

- ANTI-SEMITISM AND THE HOLOCAUST: The most distressing topic; fiction is often used as a way to talk about the unspeakable

- ISRAEL: A brief history of Zionism, and a discussion of the relationship between Diaspora Jews and the land of Israel

- THEOLOGY AND PRAYER: Jewish concepts of God, Jewish ways of talking to God

- COVENANT AND "CHOSENNESS": The Jewish contract with God

Some students find the assigned reading difficult, while others feel less than challenged by it. If you seek more depth in your reading or want to learn more about a specific topic, ask the teacher for a bibliography. Although your sponsoring rabbi is probably better able to tailor a reading list to your needs, teachers in large classes welcome and respond to feedback. In one case, when several students in a big "Introduction to Judaism" class expressed interest in learning more about Kabbalah and Jewish spirituality, the rabbi offered a mini-course at lunchtime in the conference room of a downtown law firm, where one of the students worked.

If you feel the need for a more sophisticated or rigorous academic introduction to Judaism, there are many other opportunities for study. Synagogues, Jewish community centers,[8] and other organizations offer all kinds of adult education lectures and courses, many of which are open to the general public. Colleges and universities offer Jewish Studies courses. Joining a synagogue's Shabbat morning Torah study group is another way to both study with and participate in the Jewish community.

Again, signing up for a conversion class does not mean you've made an ironclad decision to become a Jew. Indeed, most such courses avoid the term "conversion" in their titles (e.g., "Introduction to Judaism," "The Path of Torah," "Jewish, Alive, and American") so as to appeal not only to students for conversion but also born-Jews who want to learn the basics and non-Jewish spouses who simply want to know more about their partner's tradition.

LEARNING HEBREW: Hebrew is the universal and sacred language of Judaism—the language of the Bible, the prayer book, and the land of Israel.[9] Most conversion classes include a few sessions on reading Hebrew, but no one can learn to speak or read any language—much less one that requires memorizing a whole new alphabet and is read from right to left—in so short a time. Introductory Hebrew lessons are intended only to familiarize you with the Hebrew *alef-bet* (alphabet) and the sounds and vocabulary of commonly used blessings, so that you can begin to feel more comfortable at synagogue services.

With this brief introduction under your belt, your rabbi will encourage you to continue studying the language. Beginning and prayer-book Hebrew classes are a regular part of most synagogue adult education programs and daylong Hebrew-reading "marathons" can provide a great jump start. A semester of weekly or biweekly classes may be all you need to grasp the rudiments, although many people find they need to take several beginner-level classes before they "get it." Audiocassettes can be helpful, and many people learn by following along with their children's lessons.

Of course, the best way to learn any language is by spending time in the country where it's spoken. Outside of going to Israel, the next best method of learning Hebrew is to attend an *ulpan*, an intensive language instruction course developed in the 1940s for immigrants to the newly formed state of Israel, and now offered in colleges and Jewish community centers throughout North America. *Ulpan* requires a fairly substantial time commitment, but adults can learn Hebrew as an access language (for reading purposes) with a much more modest commitment of time.

Although learning Hebrew is important, don't let it become a stumbling block. It is not essential to learn Hebrew to become a Jew; indeed, the vast majority of American Jews-by-birth cannot speak or read Hebrew. Learning Hebrew is part of learning about Judaism—an ongoing process and a lifelong goal. So if someone asks if you know Hebrew, a good answer is "Not yet." In the meanwhile, most prayers are transliterated—that is, the Hebrew sounds are spelled out in the Latin alphabet.

And don't worry that you're "faking it" when, for example, you recite the blessings at your *mikvah* or over the Friday night candles without being able to read or translate every word. Rote memorization is part of all language acquisition.

LEARNING BY DOING: Although Judaism has a rich intellectual tradition, you can't become a Jew in a classroom. Judaism is a way of life, full of melodies, foods, jokes, vacation destinations, retail experiences, and emotional contradictions. All courses for conversion now include small-group sessions run by social workers and psychologists who lead discussions on a range of issues: from family dynamics, to concerns about holiday celebrations (especially Christmas), to fears about becoming a victim of anti-Semitism.

Many people find these sessions to be enormously helpful and reassuring, and lasting friendships have been forged in them. It's good to find out that you're not the only one having nightmares about Nazis, or mourning the loss of your Christmas tree, or worrying about being too blond (or African or Asian or Irish) to ever fit into the Jewish community. Participants help each other by sharing strategies and trading information and building a Jewish community—however temporary.

In addition to attending group discussions and classes, having meetings with the rabbi, and reading, you will also be urged to practice "doing Jewish" and being Jewish, including some, many, or all of the following: attending regular worship services, celebrating Jewish holidays, subscribing to a Jewish newspaper or magazine, buying a Jewish calendar, becoming familiar with Jewish communal organizations and charities. Some rabbis suggest that prospective converts attend services in synagogues of different Jewish denominations—Reform, Conservative, Reconstructionist, and Orthodox—to get a firsthand view of the varieties of Jewish worship.

Some other suggestions for experimenting with Jewish practice and experiencing Jewish culture:

- Observe one full Shabbat. For twenty-five hours, do no work—not even the laundry. Attend services, read and relax, but don't go shopping or cook. If you have children, do something fun together as a family on Saturday afternoon.
- Attend a synagogue-sponsored Shabbat retreat for a sense of what a complete communal day of rest can be.
- Try to keep kosher in a basic way for a month as a way to infuse one of the most basic of human needs with Jewish content. At home and when you eat out, avoid all shellfish and pork products, don't mix meat and milk, read labels in the supermarket and don't buy foods prepared with lard.

- Plan and host a holiday celebration. Run your own Passover seder.
- Go shopping in a kosher food store and a Jewish bookstore.
- Attend Jewish theater performances, Jewish choral groups, shows by touring Israeli pop stars.
- Tour the local Jewish community center.
- Attend an Israel Independence Day celebration.
- If you are a member of a congregation, get involved in a congregational program or two. Attend an adult education class or sisterhood events. Volunteer for committee work.
- Include Jewish tours and expeditions while on vacations or business trips. In New York City, visit the Lower East Side, the Jewish Museum, and Ellis Island. In Washington, go to the Holocaust Museum. In Rome, visit the ancient Jewish ghetto. Whether you find yourself in Baltimore or Bombay, try to find the oldest synagogue in the city, or make a pilgrimage to the best Jewish deli. If you're in a strange city on Shabbat, go to services at a local synagogue.[10]

If you have a Jewish partner, these kinds of "extra-curricular" learning-by-doing experiences can be especially important. As you study, attend synagogue services, go to concerts, experiment with religious observance, make new friends in class or at temple, you are creating shared Jewish memories. Your "firsts"—first Hanukkah candle-lighting (just the two of you), first taste of *kishke*, first Jewish art purchase—will become part of a shared Jewish past, part of the story you tell your friends, your children, perhaps even your grandchildren.

Mentors: In the best of all possible worlds, all converts would have terrific sponsoring rabbis, inspiring lecturers, helpful and participatory Jewish partners, supportive parents, welcoming Jewish in-laws, and lots of Jewish friends who invite you to participate in holiday and life-cycle observances.

But this is the real world, in which some sponsoring rabbis are too busy to spend enough time with you, some fiancés flatly refuse to attend conversion classes, some parents stop talking to sons or daughters who they feel are repudiating them by becoming a Jew, and some prospective Jewish in-laws are skeptical and cold. And what if you don't really know any Jews except for your partner, who had no real Jewish education to speak of? What if you're single and new in town?

If you find yourself spending a lot of time talking to the "Introduction to Judaism" teacher in the parking lot after class, you could probably use a mentor. But regardless of your particular circumstances, most converts to Judaism benefit from a relationship with a nonrelated layperson who becomes a kind of Jewish big brother or sister. Even if you feel close to your sponsoring rabbi, the rabbi is, nonetheless, a professional teacher and, in a sense, a professional Jew. A Jewish mentor, on the other hand, is someone like you who embodies the way an ordinary Jew lives a Jewish life.

A Jewish mentor is a role model who invites you to his or her house for Shabbat dinner, who sits next to you during services, who gives you a great recipe for challah or honey cake, who can translate the alphabet soup of the Jewish communal world for you. Sometimes mentors are older born-Jews who have adult children and a lifetime of Jewish memories to share. But mentors can also be Jews-by-choice who know exactly what you're going through. Whoever they are, mentors are hosts, sounding boards, and friends. If asked, they will accompany you to the *mikvah*. Unasked, they will give you a gift on the occasion of your conversion, and *kvell* (a Yiddish word that means "bask in your reflected glory") about your conversion.

Mentoring relationships sometimes develop spontaneously, but they often need to be arranged. Your rabbi may know someone in his or her congregation who would be a good match for you. Don't be shy about seeking out a mentor. Actually, you perform a *mitzvah* by giving someone else the opportunity to do the *mitzvah* of helping you find your way.

KEEPING A JOURNAL: Rabbis sometimes propose that you keep a journal while studying for conversion. This may be an offhand suggestion, such as "Some people find it useful to keep track of their thoughts and feelings," and no further mention is made of it. The rabbi may ask that you use a journal to record and focus questions for discussion, or give you specific writing assignments, such as reactions to your first meeting together and a summation just before formal conversion ceremonies.

Writing a religious or spiritual autobiography can clarify your thinking during a period of serious decision-making. Your journal can take the form of a daily diary to record reactions to classes, meetings with the rabbi, conversations with parents and friends, moments of doubt and fear, moments of comfort and mastery. But a journal is also a chance to reflect back on childhood, adolescence, and your search for meaning and a spiritual home. Writing can open the past to new interpretations as you trace the path that led you to a rabbi's study and the prospect of becoming a Jew.

A tool for reflection and self-exploration, a conversion journal is a place to wonder: What led me to Judaism? Why do I want to become a Jew? How will conversion change me? Will my parents ever forgive me? Will I ever stop missing Christmas? Is everyone staring at me in temple or am I just being paranoid?

Although most people tend to think of journals as totally private, sharing what you've written—or at least parts of it— can transform writing from an act of self-reflection into an act of self-transformation. In an unconscious echo of the Talmud's encouragement of group study, Dan Wakefield, a writer who runs spiritual autobiography workshops, says unequivocally, "Don't do it alone."[11] Sharing a journal entry with the discussion group in your conversion class—or with your rabbi or partner—almost always reveals meanings that were not apparent to you when you wrote it. The sense of community, of being on a journey with others, is one of the essential gifts of Judaism.

And journals don't have to be limited to words. Artists may find drawing or painting to be more useful, so if you're a visual thinker you might begin by sketching the road that brought you from your childhood home to the rabbi's study, then write a description of the drawing, paying attention to what each element or signpost means to you.

Sometimes it helps to have an assignment to focus on writing religious autobiography. Possible topics might include: your earliest religious memories, your first or most memorable Jewish experience, religious experiences during adolescence, a list or drawing of Christmas images.

It helps to make journal writing a regular habit. Buy yourself a special notebook and set aside ten minutes every day or even just once a week (perhaps on Friday afternoon, just before Shabbat begins) for reflection. If you discover that you like writing about your spiritual life, don't stop after the ceremonies are over. The year (or years) after becoming a Jew are at least as full of change and challenge as the year leading up to it. Use the Jewish calendar to set up a regular schedule for writing: before Shabbat every week, or at the start of each new Jewish month. Or make an annual entry during the week between Rosh Hashanah (the Jewish New Year) and Yom Kippur (the Day of Atonement), which is a traditional period of reflection.

Am I Ready?

*T*HIS QUESTION DOES NOT OCCUR TO EVERYONE. Some people know that they were meant to be Jews since childhood. Some people enter a synagogue and feel completely at home. Some people walk into the *mikvah* without a single doubt or regret.

On the other hand, if the question is pressing upon you and something in your heart says "No," listen. That is your answer—at least for now.

But for many people, the answer is not yes or no but "maybe." This puts you in an awkward spot—one foot in, one foot out. It's not a comfortable position, but it's completely normal and not a sign that you lack commitment or that Judaism is wrong for you. The fact is, you may never feel completely, utterly, confidently ready to become a Jew. "Maybe" may be as close you get. There is no external measure or sign, no report card, no blinding flash of light from on high to assure you that you've mastered the material and the time has come.

And yet, at some point your rabbi will say, "I think you are ready." Which places you squarely on a platform facing a leap of faith.

You may have been up here before. People get married without being 100 percent certain of what marriage is going to be like. Nobody who becomes a parent for the first time has any idea of how much a baby will change his or her life. All of life's major decisions are risky, dangerous, exhilarating.

The reasons for making any choice this big are never entirely cerebral. You choose Judaism because of the way your child loves Sunday school, because you've come to experience anti-Semitic remarks as personal attacks, because you love Mel Brooks, because of your relationship with your rabbi, because of the conversation at the Passover seder. Because it feels right.

Sometimes, there is an epiphany. Your rabbi might tell you that you'll be ready when you hear yourself say "us" instead of "them," "we" instead of "you." (This does not mean that you've made a terrible mistake when someday, inevitably, you slip and say "them" when you meant "us." It happens.)

One woman tells a story about jogging past a man reading a Hebrew book. She slowed down, realizing that she shared something important with this total stranger.

"Shalom," she said. He smiled and said "Shalom." The next day she called her rabbi to schedule her conversion.

For another convert, the connection was made during a visit to Yad Vashem, the Holocaust memorial in Jerusalem. Another man realized he was ready when he got into a heated argument about synagogue politics with a member of his congregation.

Not everyone experiences a dramatic moment of recognition. For many, the decision comes under pressure from an important deadline: a wedding, the birth of a baby, a bat mitzvah. In order to fully participate in the life-cycle event before you, you need to be Jewish. And that makes you ready enough.

You will not know everything you think you ought to know about Judaism, but you will know enough. You will not understand everything you think you need to understand about being a Jew, but you will understand enough. The rituals and ceremonies that mark your conversion are like a wedding, which does not celebrate the end of your engagement. A conversion, like a wedding, is just the beginning.

Choosing a Hebrew Name

The Holy One of Blessing said, "The names of proselytes are beloved unto me like the wine of libation brought upon the altar."

VAYIKRA RABBAH

As YOU NEAR THE DATE OF YOUR CONVERSION, your rabbi will suggest you start thinking about a Hebrew name, which will be used in religious and ceremonial moments of your Jewish life: when you are called to the Torah, when you are married, and when you die. It does not replace or displace the name your parents gave you at birth, it is an additional name that identifies you as a member of the Jewish people.[12]

Every Jew-by-choice has a story to tell about his or her Hebrew name:

"My older daughter thought she had veto power over my name since it would become her name, when she was called to the

Torah for her bat mitzvah. No names leaped out at me from the Torah, so I looked at a list, especially for something with a B, since my name is Brad. I chose Ben-ami, 'son of my people.' It felt right."

"Nivchara means 'chosen' or 'choice' in Hebrew, to reflect my decision to become a Jew. I added Ruth because it is she with whom I most closely identify."

"I chose Rachel. Because her life situation mirrored mine (I was a second wife, who inherited sons from the first wife), she was the character I felt most able to identify with. By accident, a lot of my dearest friends also have the name. Sharing it with them makes me feel like I'm a kind of relative!"

"I chose Isaac because I had a great-great-great grandfather whose name was Isaac."

"My name is Moshe Isaac. The *M* in Moshe is for Mark, which is my name. I've always loved Moses—for his actions and his courage. Also, I love water and Moses means 'drawn from the water.' I love the ocean, I love to swim. As for Isaac, my future father-in-law always wanted a son and would have given him the name Isaac. His three daughters didn't give him that chance, so I did."

"My Hebrew name is Alizah, which means 'joy.' In every way I feel myself to be a descendant of Ruth."

The power of names and naming is a recurrent theme in Jewish tradition. Adam's job in Eden was to name the beasts of the field, the birds of the air, and every living thing. Because the Hebrew for "word," *davar,* also means "thing," the story suggests that Adam was an active participant in the process of creation. Choosing a Hebrew name is a way of creating and naming your new Jewish self. It is a way to give voice to who you really are and who you hope to become.

In the Torah, name changes occur at moments of profound and far-reaching spiritual transformation. When Abram and Sarai decide to become partners in God's covenant, their names are changed. With the addition of the Hebrew letter *hay*—which is considered especially holy since it appears twice in YHVH, the unpronounceable name of God—Abram becomes Abraham and Sarai becomes Sarah. Jacob is renamed as Israel after wrestling with a divine messenger.

Your Hebrew name gives you the chance to express something about who you are as an individual, but it also places you within the ranks of the Jewish people. According to the rabbis of the Talmud, the Jews enslaved in Egypt had all but forgotten God, but because they held fast to their language, to the practice of circumcision, and to their Hebrew names, they were saved from total assimilation.

HOW TO PICK A HEBREW NAME: In the past, all male converts were encouraged to take the name Abraham and all female converts were urged to become Sarah.[13] In practice, converts have always selected Hebrew names that speak to them personally; Ruth has long been a favorite for obvious reasons. Most converts choose a biblical name. There are twenty-eight hundred personal names in the Hebrew Bible, and although fewer than 5 percent of those are in current use,[14] all of them are yours to consider.

Many of the names in the Bible are theophoric, meaning that they exalt God. Names with the prefixes or suffixes *el, eli, ya,* and *yahu* all refer to the Holy One: Elisha—God is my salvation; Raphael—God has healed; Gamliel—God is my reward. Others describe the circumstances of birth or a person's historical role. Chava, Hebrew for Eve, comes from the root word for "life," *chai.* The name Isaac comes from the word for "laughter," because his mother laughed to learn she would bear a child at her advanced age. The Bible also contains many names that refer to the natural universe: Deborah—bee; Jonah—dove; Tamar—palm tree. Many modern Israeli names continue this tradition: Tal and Tali—dew; Alon or Alona—oak; Oren—fir tree.

The lexicon of Hebrew names was not handed down from Mount Sinai; it has grown and changed throughout history and in response to local customs and fashions. Take, for example, the quintessentially Jewish name Esther, which is Persian in origin and shares its root with the fertility goddess, Ishtar. When the state of Israel was founded, in 1948, scores of new Hebrew names were invented and many old ones reclaimed. Your rabbi should be able to provide you with guidance, lists, even suggestions. Once you find one or two names that you especially like, you might ask the rabbi to help you find some texts about the biblical character or name you've selected.

But you may not have to look any further than your own given name for inspiration. Some names translate beautifully: Regina or Gina, which means "queen," can give rise to Malkah, which also means "queen." If your parents named you David, David (pronounced "Dah-*veed*") can be your Hebrew name as well. The biblical precedent for this practice is clear: Ruth did not change her name.

Many converts follow the contemporary American custom of selecting a Hebrew name based on the initial letter or sound of their English name. Thus, Robert chooses Reuben, and Mary selects Miriam. But don't feel obligated by an accident of the alphabet. Since Jewish babies are usually named after parents or grandparents,[15] some converts choose a name to honor someone in their own lives. Some rabbis feel strongly that the person you honor should be a Jewish teacher or mentor, or even a historical figure you find inspiring.

But there's no rule that you have to find an orthographic or historical connection between your name and your Hebrew name. This is an area of Jewish practice where there are few rules or customs, so find a name that feels right and has meaning for you. And you needn't limit yourself to just one name; it is increasingly common to choose two or even three. It sounds very impressive to be called to the Torah as Sarah Ora Hadass bat Avraham v'Sarah.

FAMILY NAMES: No Jew is simply David or Leah. David's *ketubah*, or marriage contract, will read David ben Moshe v'Rivka, David the son of Moses and Rebecca. When Leah is called to read from the Torah, she will be called Leah bat

Raphael v'Miriam, Leah the daughter of Raphael and Miriam. Whatever name you choose, when it is used, it will be attached to the name of your Jewish father and, in virtually all liberal congregations, your Jewish mother.

Jews-by-choice are traditionally given the names of the very first Jewish parents, Avraham Avienu (Abraham our Father) and Sarah Imenu (Sarah our Mother).[16] This nomenclature makes spiritual sense in that converts can claim a special kinship to the progenitors of the entire Jewish people, who themselves were Jews-by-choice. To be identified as the child of Abraham and Sarah is to be given "the crown of a good name," a name to be borne with pride, and deserving of honor.

Nevertheless, some Jews-by-choice dislike this custom, which identifies them as converts. As one woman explained, "I felt for a long time that whenever I went up to read Torah, that name put a flashing sign up above my head that says 'convert.' It was a moment of feeling left out or excluded at precisely the moment I feel I should belong."

This woman decided to change her ancestral names: "When I am called to the Torah, I say that my name is Rachel bat Eliyahu v'Miriam. Eliyahu is for a rabbi I studied with, and also for the prophet Elijah, who answers unanswerable questions. And Miriam is because I've always loved her character in the Bible."

Choosing one's own ancestors in this fashion is a new custom, and controversial; it is something to discuss with your rabbi.

Family names can be complicated if one of a convert's parents is Jewish and the other is not. Custom varies in such cases. Often, only the Jewish parent's name is used (i.e., Rachel bat Moshe), but sometimes the non-Jewish parent's name is "translated" (Rachel bat Moshe v'Hannah) or the non-Jewish parent's name is stated in English (Rachel bat Moshe v'Ellen). This, too, is a decision to discuss with your rabbi.

Whatever your name, your status as a Jew-by-choice is not hereditary. Your children's names will refer only to your Hebrew name, without any reference to conversion. Like all grandparents, Abraham and Sarah recede into history and memory.

Two helpful resources when looking for a Hebrew name: *The New Jewish Baby Book* by Anita Diamant (Jewish Lights Publishing, 1993), which includes a list of names in current use and an essay on the history of Jewish names; *The Complete Dictionary of English and Hebrew Names* by Alfred J. Kolatch (Jonathan David Publishers, 1984), which is the most comprehensive list available and includes a Hebrew vocabulary index so you can find a name that reflects a particular quality, such as "love" or "strength."

PART III

Rituals

and

Ceremonies

*W*HAT DOES A *MIKVAH* LOOK LIKE?

I'M ALREADY CIRCUMCISED, SO WHY DO I HAVE TO UNDERGO A RITUAL REENACTMENT OF IT?

*W*HAT IS THE *BET DIN* GOING TO ASK ME?

*H*OW CAN I INCLUDE MY PARENTS IN THIS TRANSITION OF MY LIFE?

*W*ILL MY FAMILY EVER ACCEPT MY KOREAN-BORN SON AS A JEW?

*A*FTER MONTHS OR YEARS OF THOUGHT, STUDY, experimentation, soul-searching, conversation, argument, doubt, and growth, you are ready to make it official. Becoming a Jew—like being a Jew—is not an entirely intellectual process. The next steps are physical, mystical, and joyous. And as in all Jewish life-cycle events, conversion is enacted with rituals, ceremonies, and celebrations that take place on three related levels—personal, communal, and familial.

The rituals are most personal. According to Jewish law, it takes more than a verbal affirmation to become a Jew, so through *mikvah* (immersion in a ritual bath), *milah* (the covenant of circumcision), and the choice of a Hebrew name, you undertake intimate acts of renewal and rebirth that are truly comprehensible only after the fact. Virtually all converts report that *mikvah* is one of the most powerful experiences of their lives: "I felt so sweet when I came out of the *mikvah*, I didn't want to wash for a week," said one woman. Men who undergo *hatafat dam brit* voice no regrets. "It was so real," said one man, attempting to name something ineffable.

Ceremonies that welcome a new Jew into the house of Israel affirm the mutual commitment of individual and community. When you stand on the *bimah* facing a congregation of your fellow Jews holding the Torah in your arms, you claim your place among the people of Israel, and your community acknowledges that it is forever changed by your presence.

The Covenant of Circumcision

*This is my covenant which you are to keep, between
me and you and your seed after you: every male among
you shall be circumcised.
You shall circumcise the flesh of your foreskin,
so that it may serve as the sign of the covenant
between me and you.*

GENESIS 17:10–11

HE COVENANT (*BRIT*) OF CIRCUMCISION (*MILAH*)
is a physical, permanent sign of the relationship between the
Jewish people and God. Jewish parents have fulfilled this, one
of the most mysterious and difficult of all biblical commandments for four thousand years. And in every generation, male
converts to Judaism have done the same. Although most male
converts to Judaism today are already circumcised, and even
though some liberal rabbis do not require *brit milah* of uncircumcised men, this *mitzvah* is central to Jewish history and
identity.

Circumcision is not an easy topic to think or talk about.
Certainly, if God had asked Abraham to remove a flap of skin
from his heel and from the heels of all the males of his house-

hold as a permanent sign of the covenant, *brit milah* would not be such an emotionally charged practice, and it might well have been abandoned as irrelevant. But because the mark of the covenant is surgically imprinted on the penis, the stakes seem enormous. With *milah,* sexuality comes under the purview of holiness and the biological act of reproduction becomes an explicitly Jewish promise for the next generation. According to the Midrash, "the Jewish people was saved by God thanks to the merit of the observance of circumcision."[1] Even Benedict Spinoza, the seventeenth-century Jewish philosopher who was excommunicated by a court of rabbis for his unorthodox beliefs, declared that the practice of *brit milah* alone would ensure the survival of the Jewish people. In the words of one contemporary Orthodox rabbi, "The ritual is demanding; the meaning abstract; the consequence of its observance was often persecution. But it remains tenaciously observed among Jews, the mark of unity in a world of assimilation and dispersal."[2]

The circumcision of newborn sons and of male converts has been an unbroken tradition from the beginning of Jewish history. However, circumcision was never unique to the Jewish people. Even in antiquity, Egyptians, Phoenicians, and Moabites circumcised their sons. For the ancient Hebrews, however, the rite was not used as a test of courage and fortitude for adolescent boys. The circumcision of eight-day-old infants[3] began and remains an act of consecration and a sign of identity.

The importance of circumcision is a recurrent theme in the Bible. Abraham circumcised himself before he could become the father of the Jewish people. Moses' wife, Zipporah (a Midianite woman), earned accolades from the rabbis because she took it upon herself to circumcise her son when Moses did not do it himself.[4] In a later generation, the prophet Elijah exhorted his contemporaries to return to the covenant of Abraham, which they had abandoned.

During the first century C.E., early Christians debated whether conversion to Christianity required circumcision—in other words, whether a man had to be a Jew before he could become a Christian. When the anticircumcision opinion prevailed, the two faiths split irrevocably. Roman law subsequently made it illegal to perform circumcision for the purpose of conversion to Judaism.

The centrality of *brit milah* has made it a target of anti-Semitic edicts through the ages. Antiochus Epiphanes (the villain of the Hanukkah story, 175–164 B.C.E.) enacted the first recorded prohibition against circumcision. Thousands of years later in Nazi Germany, the mark of the covenant was often a death warrant.[5]

But even though Jews have performed *brit milah* with amazing consistency through the generations, the meaning of the *mitzvah* has been debated all the while. The rabbis examined every aspect of the biblical account of Abraham's circumcision to try to discern God's purpose; the word *orlah*, for instance, inspired great speculation. *Orlah* is translated as "foreskin," but since the word can also refer to any barrier standing in the way of a beneficial result, *orlah* was seen as a metaphor for things that prevent people from hearing or understanding God. *Brit milah* thus symbolically affirms the ability of men to change their very nature in order to be closer to God.

The rabbis had many theories as to why God demanded such an intimate sacrifice. Much has been made of the irreversibility of *milah*; the permanence of the covenant sealed in the flesh is a constant reminder that there is no going back on a contract with God.[6] Some of the sages believed that God required circumcision as a curb on the sexual drive that would otherwise lure men away from God.

Although many "whys" have been offered, there is at least one clear "why not." Despite evidence of its medical benefits,[7] Jews have never performed circumcision on their infant sons for reasons of health. Moses Maimonides, the twelfth-century rabbi, philosopher, and physician, explained, "No one should circumcise himself or his sons for any other reasons but for pure faith. Circumcision is the symbol of the covenant which Abraham made in connection with the belief in God's unity."[8]

Ultimately, circumcision is an act of faith that defies a strictly logical explication. But it is, undeniably, a sign of connection to the most ancient past of the Jewish people and to its future as well.

BRIT MILAH AND CONVERSION: *Brit milah* is sometimes referred to as the covenant of Abraham, who circumcised himself in order to become a Jew. According to the Midrash, the timing of Abraham's act had special significance.

Abraham was forty-eight-years old when he came to know his creator. Yet he was not commanded to circumcise himself at that time and waited until he was much older—ninety-nine years of age.

Why? In order not to close the door upon proselytes, however advanced in years.[9]

Actually, there is no explicit commandment in the Torah requiring circumcision (or immersion) for proselytes. The Talmud—the Oral Law—is where the laws and debates about initiation rites are found. There was general, though by no means universal, agreement among the rabbis that male converts must undergo both circumcision and *mikvah*. (Women only have to immerse.)[10]

Despite the pain and risk that attended adult circumcision prior to the invention of anesthetics and antiseptic practice, adult men in every generation have submitted to circumcision in order to become Jews. Today, Orthodox and Conservative Jews still require circumcision or *hatafat dam brit*, its ritual reenactment. The Reform movement has accepted converts without *milah* or *mikvah* since 1892, a decision based in part on the absence of biblical law and also upon minority positions in the Talmud that argued circumcision was not the sine qua non for conversion.[11] While the Reform and Reconstructionist movements do not require *milah* or *mikvah*, an increasing number of rabbis affiliated with both do make it a condition for their conversion candidates, so check with your rabbi.

Given the historical and religious significance of *brit milah*, the idea that an uncircumcised man can be a Jew seems like a logical impossibility. However, the case has been made that, like the uncircumcised Russian Jews who embraced their birthright after immigrating to the United States or Israel, uncircumcised converts may be seen as Jews in need of circumcision—but Jews nonetheless.

HATAFAT DAM BRIT—REENACTING THE RITUAL: For much of this century, nearly all American baby boys underwent circumcision as a health measure, a fact that made adult circumcision unnecessary for most male converts.[12] However, medical circumcision is not the same as *brit milah*. The removal of the foreskin is only one part of the ritual, which must be performed with the intention of entering a boy or man into the covenant of Israel. Thus, Jewish law requires that circumcised converts undergo a ritual reenactment called *hatafat dam brit*. *Hatafat* means "drop"; *dam* means "blood."

The ritual requires that a single drop of blood be taken from the site of the circumcision—more precisely, from the corona of skin that surrounds the head (or glans) of the penis. The person performing the *hatafat dam brit* applies an alcohol swab to the area and then pricks the skin either with a hypodermic needle or a sterile lancet. The blood is collected on a gauze pad, which may then be shown to three witnesses.

The ritual is generally scheduled days or even hours before *mikvah*. Typically, your rabbi will make all the necessary arrangements for *hatafat dam brit*, which is usually performed in a physician's office, though it can take place in any private place. The convert does not need to fully disrobe. There is no cutting, no suturing, and no subsequent bleeding. The entire procedure takes only a few moments.

Hatafat dam brit is generally performed by a *mohel*, a ritual circumciser. (The Yiddish pronunciation is "moil," the Hebrew is "mo-*hail*.") A *mohel* is someone trained to perform both the covenantal prayers and the surgical procedure of *brit milah*. Traditionally, one becomes a *mohel* by apprenticeship with an established practitioner, but since the 1980s the Reform and Conservative movements have recruited, trained, and certified licensed physicians to serve as *mohelim* for the liberal Jewish community.

Rabbis and *mohelim* tend to insist that *hatafat dam brit* is painless. Converts allow that although it's over in a second, "painless" is not an altogether accurate description, though some men find the alcohol wipe more irritating than the jab. Physicians who perform *hatafat dam brit* sometimes prescribe a numbing cream, which is applied to the area a few hours earlier.

Despite the minor physical and not-so-minor psychological discomfort (the anticipation is always worse than the event), converts invariably say that the importance of the ritual far outweighed any pain. And as one man said, "You wouldn't believe the kind of respect it earned me from my mother-in-law."

There is no liturgy for the ritual of *hatafat dam brit*. Some *mohelim* recite a blessing before drawing the drop of blood, but others do not. Afterward, the witnesses, *mohel*, rabbi, and convert may say the blessing over wine—a universal feature of all Jewish rituals. However, given the emotional and ritual importance of the moment, some rabbis and *mohe-*

lim now include new as well as old blessings and even a brief ceremony. (See pages 110–11.)

BRIT MILAH—ADULT CIRCUMCISION FOR CONVERSION: The requirement of circumcision for male converts has undoubtedly limited Judaism's appeal to outsiders. The prospect of submitting one's penis to the knife is physically daunting and psychologically traumatic. And yet, there have always been men willing to undergo *brit milah* in order to become full members of the Jewish community.

Of course, modern medicine greatly minimizes the danger and pain associated with circumcision, and since urologists and some general surgeons routinely perform circumcisions for medical reasons, the procedure itself is fairly easy to arrange.

Only an experienced urologist or general surgeon should undertake an adult circumcision, and several of the *mohelim* certified by the Conservative and Reform movements are qualified in these fields. A Jewish surgeon who is not a *mohel* can perform *brit milah* by saying the blessing before he does the surgery. If the only available surgeon is a non-Jew, a *mohel* (or indeed any Jew) may say the blessing. Finally, a medical circumcision can be performed and then followed, at a later date, by *hatafat dam brit*.[14] Your rabbi should be able to refer you to a physician/*mohel*, or help set up a kosher alternative.

Adult circumcision is performed as day surgery. The procedure takes about thirty minutes, and patients are sent home as soon as the anesthesia wears off. Local, spinal, or general anesthesia may be used, depending upon the patient's anxiety

Hatafat Dam Brit

The *mohel* greets the convert:

בָּרוּךְ הַבָּא בְּשֵׁם יְיָ.

Baruch ha–ba b'shem Adonai

Blessed are you who come in God's name.

The convert reads:

הִנְנִי מוּכָן

Hineni Muchan

Here am I, ready,

God of Abraham,

Reverent before Your commanding Presence and
the sacred tradition into which I now bring
my soul and my body.

As I have overcome obstacles and doubts,
ambivalence, and fear

to stand before You this day,

so do I, with love and devotion, begin a new way
of life

dedicated to Torah and her blessings.

Receive me into the covenant of the people Israel.

Help me to find a new home in the mystery of
Your covenant.

Amen.[13]

The *mohel* recites the blessing:

בָּרוּךְ אַתָּה יְיָ, אֱלֹהֵינוּ מֶלֶךְ הָעוֹלָם,
אֲשֶׁר קִדְּשָׁנוּ בְּמִצְוֹתָיו, וְצִוָּנוּ לָמוּל אֶת הַגֵּרִים.

Blessed are You, Adonai our God, Ruler of the
Universe, Who sanctifies us with commandments
and commands us regarding the circumcision of the
convert.

The *mohel* takes a drop of blood. He hands the convert a spice box—a reviving reminder of the sweetness of Jewish life.

    After the convert is dressed, the *mohel,* rabbi,
and one other Jewish witness raise a glass of wine and
recite the blessing over wine, and the *shehehiyanu:*

בָּרוּךְ אַתָּה יְיָ, אֱלֹהֵינוּ מֶלֶךְ הָעוֹלָם,
שֶׁהֶחֱיָנוּ וְקִיְּמָנוּ וְהִגִּיעָנוּ לַזְּמַן הַזֶּה.

Blessed are You, Adonai our God, Ruler of the
Universe, for giving us life, for sustaining us, for
enabling us to reach this day.

level. Most men return to work the day after circumcision, with a prescription for a mild analgesic to alleviate postoperative pain. Dissolvable sutures are used so there are no stitches to remove; however, the urologist will want to check on the healing process after about two weeks. Swelling and discoloration persist for a week or two, and intercourse is prohibited for three to four weeks. Complications are rare, minor, and easily treated.

The religious ritual for an adult *brit milah* is minimal: the surgeon/*mohel* recites the blessing for the circumcision of converts prior to making the first incision, and a *bet din* must witness the *brit* by viewing a drop of blood from the incision.

Final Exam: The Bet Din

*J*UDAISM IS A FUNDAMENTALLY COMMUNAL religious system, which is to say that you aren't a Jew unless other Jews say that you are. When you and your rabbi decide that you are ready, the rabbi will convene a religious court or tribunal called a *bet din* (literally, "house of judgment"), which represents the Jewish community in determining your sincerity and readiness.[15]

Most converts dread the prospect of facing a *bet din*. Regardless of how many times your rabbi tells you not to worry, it's hard not to feel anxious about appearing before a court of law. But there really is no need to "cram" for your *bet din*. This is not a Ph.D. dissertation defense and no one is out to stump you or make you look foolish. Your rabbi will not convene a *bet din* unless he or she is certain that you are ready.

Even so, the *bet din* is not a *pro forma* process that automatically ends with acceptance. Although it is extremely rare, candidates are sometimes turned away. Rabbis with decades of experience can recall only one or two occasions when a person was turned away. In those cases, the person expressed some grave theological reservation (one woman said she felt her decision to become a Jew meant that she would go to hell) or was clearly upset about the pain and conflict the conversion would create among family members. Prospective converts who refer to "you" and "them" rather than "me" and "us" when talking about Jews and Judaism also signal a lack of identification and sincerity.

But the goal of the people who serve on *bet din*s for conversion is not to keep you out. In the words of the Reconstructionist Rabbinical Association's guidelines on conversion, "The *bet din* experience should be warm and memorable."

Usually, the *bet din* is comprised of three ordained rabbis; however, other knowledgeable adult Jewish laypeople or community leaders may also serve. In some cases, converts know all three members of their *bet din*, but sometimes only one face will be familiar. Given the difficulties of scheduling, it's often necessary to convene a *bet din* for more than one convert at a time.

One way to lower your anxiety about appearing before a *bet din* is to bring someone with you. Many rabbis welcome spouses, fiancés, or partners to watch the proceedings. If there are other people you want to be present (mentors, members of your congregation, supportive family members), ask your sponsoring rabbi if they can come, too. The answer may depend on the size of the room where the *bet din* is to be held as much as anything else, but the answer will probably be "Of course."

There is no one-size-fits-all "test" for converts, no list of mandatory questions, and no minimum score. The three people before you are charged with making a serious but profoundly subjective evaluation of your sincerity.[16] In other words, while this won't be a tough exam, it's not going to be an easy conversation, either. You will be asked to explain yourself.

Although no two *bet din*s ask the same questions, most tend to be subjective and open-ended, such as:

- Why are you converting to Judaism at this point in your life?

- If I came to your house, what would show me that it's a Jewish home?

- What aspects of Judaism are already a part of your life?

- Describe the seder you went to last Passover.

- What do your parents think about your decision to become a Jew?

- Do you feel any regret about putting aside Jesus?

- What are your plans and goals for your children's Jewish upbringing?

- Which of the *mitzvot* mean the most to you right now?

- How do you feel about anti-Semitism, and about subjecting your children to its dangers?[17]

The *bet din* may also ask questions that require cognitive knowledge about Judaism. While you will not be quizzed on dates, you do need a grasp of the basic vocabulary of Jewish life in order to be able to answer such questions as:

- What part of *havdalah* do you find most meaningful?

- Tell us something about your Shabbat observance goals.

- How do you intend to make *tzedakah* part of your life?

After you have answered several questions, the members of the *bet din* may simply nod at one another and tell you that they are satisfied with your knowledge and commitment. However, some rabbis prefer that you leave the room for a few minutes while they deliberate.

The court may then ask you to read and sign a statement of commitment or simply to respond to a few vowlike statements or questions that formalize your intention to observe the *mitzvot,* to raise children as Jews, to give up any previously held religious beliefs that conflict with Judaism, and to attest that you are acting entirely of your own free will. The form of this statement varies from movement to movement and even from one *bet din* to the next. Sometimes, these questions are asked later in the *mikvah* or at a conversion ceremony in the synagogue.

CERTIFICATES: It is the responsibility of the *bet din* to sign a certificate of conversion. Your rabbi will provide the document, which officially certifies that the requirements for conversion, as understood by the undersigned, were met and witnessed. At the point of signing the certificate, you will be asked what Hebrew name you have chosen and it will be entered on a document that certifies your conversion, which is signed by the members of the *bet din*. The rabbinical associations of the Reform and Conservative movements both publish these documents in Hebrew and in English, and while most rabbis make use of the movement certificates, some produce documents of their own.

Generally, the original is given to the new Jew and a copy is made for the synagogue's files. Reform rabbis also send a copy to the American Jewish Archives at the Hebrew Union College (3101 Clifton Avenue, Cincinnati, OH 45220).

Conversion certificates tend to be simple, unadorned, and legalistic in appearance. However, the Reform movement does publish a handsome calligraphed document, in Hebrew and English, with an attractive border of vines and flowers. (For more information, call the UAHC Press toll-free at 1-888-489-8242.) And while they have yet to become the occasion for the variety and array of original artwork and ornamentation seen on *ketubot* (Jewish marriage contracts), it is only a matter of time before Jews-by-choice and their communities apply the principle of *hiddur mitzvah*—the adornment of holiness—to these important religious documents.

Mikvah:
A River from Eden

*And a river went out of Eden to water the garden and
from there it split into four headwaters.*

GENESIS 2:10

*As soon as the convert immerses and emerges,
he is a Jew in every respect.*

YEVAMOT 47B

THE HEALING AND SPIRITUALLY CLEANSING PROP-
erties of water are known to all spiritual traditions and all
lovers of beaches, lakes, and rivers. According to Talmudic interpretation, all the water in the world has its source in the
river that emerged from Eden,[18] so it is no wonder that water
has the potential to change us—to make us feel new and
whole. In Judaism, that essential insight is formalized in the
rituals of the *mikvah*.[19]

Mikvah, Hebrew for a pool or gathering of water, refers
both to natural bodies of *mayyim hayyim* (living water) and to
indoor pools created specifically for the purpose of *tevilah* (ritual immersion), which is required of all converts. The building
that houses the ritual bath is also called a *mikvah*.

Mikva'ot (the plural of *mikvah*) have been part of the Jewish landscape for two thousand years. One of the oldest—twenty centuries old—was discovered in the military fortress at Masada in Israel. According to the Talmud, Jewish communities are required to build a *mikvah* even before they build a school or a synagogue.

The primary reason to build *mikva'ot* is for women to ritually purify themselves following their menstrual cycles, according to the laws of ritual family purity.[20] It is also traditional for brides to immerse before their weddings, and some Jews (both male and female) also use the *mikvah* to prepare themselves for Passover and for Yom Kippur, the Day of Atonement.

Through most of Jewish history, immersion in a *mikvah* has been the universal ritual of conversion to Judaism. Since the first or second century C.E., women and men, adults and children, have submerged themselves in water, recited prayers, and emerged as Jews. When you walk into the water of the *mikvah,* you follow in their wake. You also enter a Jewish institution and partake of an ancient and elemental Jewish experience that is utterly foreign to the vast majority of liberal born-Jews.

If you are converting under the auspices of a Conservative or Orthodox rabbi, *mikvah* is not a choice but a requirement. Reform and Reconstructionist rabbis strongly urge (and some require) their students to do *mitzvah* as well.[21]

Mikvah is an experience of the body and the soul. Although preparing for conversion is largely an intellectual activity, immersion is an altogether physical act, a ritual enactment of commitment, a spiritual leap. *Mikvah* defies logic; after all, how can getting wet change your life? And yet, as most Jews-by-choice will tell you, it is a transforming emotional experience. Floating in the *mikvah*—every limb, every pore, every strand of hair covered by waters as warm as those of your mother's womb—you are held in a primal embrace and emerge, in a way, reborn.

Immersion can be understood as a personal experience of Sinai—of revelation. Although there is no mention of *mikvah* in the Torah itself, later interpreters used the story of the giving of the Torah at Mount Sinai to create a biblical precedent for ritual purification through water. Immediately before the Ten Commandments were given to Israel, God tells Moses to sanctify the people and have them "wash their garments."[22] Just as the Jewish people purified themselves before receiving the Torah, the convert enters the *mikvah* before being called upon to hold the Torah in his or her congregation.

You share this experience of Sinai with Jews-by-choice of every generation, all the way back to the "mixed multitude"—the non-Israelites who followed Moses into the desert in search of freedom—mentioned in the Torah.[23] As one Jew-by-choice put it, "When you lead a Passover seder, you have all of the generations of your Jewish family, since Sinai, standing behind you. When I lead the seder, I feel as though I have all of the generations of Jews who entered the *mikvah* standing right beside me."

Mikvah is not about cleansing sins or a rebirth that blots out your life prior to conversion. And yet, entering the water does offer an opportunity to redefine yourself in fundamental ways. Since the days of the ancient Temple, *mikvah* has been used to signify changes in status—within the community, within personal relationships, and within one's own heart. Immersion is a way to mark the transition between being an unmarried person to being a bride or groom. Immersing before Shabbat or Yom Kippur bespeaks a desire to start over, to do better.[24] For Jews-by-choice, *mikvah* is the ritual threshold that leads into the house of Israel.

A GUIDE TO THE *MIKVAH*: Community *mikva'ot* are run, for the most part, by the Orthodox community for the Orthodox community. Most employ women colloquially known as "*mikvah* ladies," who hold the keys to the building, witness female immersions, and maintain a supply of clean towels. A fee is charged to everyone who uses the facility.

No two *mikva'ot* look the same. Some are located in modern facilities built for the purpose, but many are housed in renovated dwellings, synagogues, schools, or even apartment buildings. If possible, arrange for a tour of the *mikvah* in advance of your conversion, but at the very least, get someone to give you a complete description of the *mikvah* you'll be using.[25]

According to Jewish law, conversions must take place on weekdays (not on Shabbat or holidays), during daylight hours. Your rabbi will tell you where the local *mikvah* is located, make an appointment for you (women should be sure that they are not scheduled for a day when they are menstruating), and inform you of the cost. Either the rabbi will collect the fee from you in advance or you will pay the *mikvah* lady yourself on the day of your immersion.

As much as *mikva'ot* vary on the outside, the pools themselves conform to standards set forth in the Talmud. A *mikvah* must be permanent, not portable, and built either into the ground or within a building. It must hold a minimum of twenty-four cubic feet of water—about two hundred gallons—and be deep enough for the water to rise above the waist of an average-height adult. Most modern *mikva'ot* are tiled and look like small, square hot tubs. Seven steps lead down into the lukewarm water, with a handrail for safety.

The water of the *mikvah* is also strictly regulated. There must be a certain proportion of natural water—usually rainwater—that has been transported to the pool via natural flow. This is then diluted with tap water, and the mixture is chemically treated for cleanliness.

The water in a *mikvah* is not considered holy. It is simply water, the natural portion of which symbolizes the source of all water (Eden), and thus the source of life. What sanctifies the *mikvah* is the intention of the person who enters the water.

The waters of a *mikvah* are not intended to clean the body. Indeed, before anyone is permitted into the pool, he or she must prepare with a thorough cleansing. Adjoining the ritual bath, you will find a fully equipped bathroom with tub, shower, sink, and towels. Your rabbi will give you a list of ablutions (shower or bathe, shampoo hair, brush and floss teeth, and remove contact lenses, jewelry, bandages, etc.). There will probably be a list posted in the bathroom as well, reminding you to remove nail polish, dental appliances, and anything else that might get between your skin and the water. The idea here is not to keep the *mikvah* clean but to permit the water access to every part and pore of your body.

In the best of cases, you will have plenty of time to get ready at the *mikvah* in a leisurely, thoughtful manner. However, most people do feel a time pressure since the *bet din* is waiting. Even so, try to take a few extra minutes to prepare yourself. (See the section on *kavannot* later in this chapter.)

Although the rules for immersion require that you be completely naked—in the presence of witnesses, no less—modesty is carefully protected at the *mikvah*. A robe or sheet will be provided so that you can enter the water discreetly. Only one person needs to actually see you in the water, and then only to check that you immerse completely.

However, because the addition of a new Jew is a communal concern, the community must be represented by a *bet din,* a tribunal of witnesses that is empowered to make legal judgments. In the interest of modesty, the *bet din* is not required to see you immerse. They may take the word of an attendant for your immersion, but they do have to hear you recite the blessings and answers to any questions that the rabbi may ask while you are in the water.

THE RITUAL: As in all other Jewish life-cycle rituals, the formal liturgy here is very brief. The core of the ceremony consists of two Hebrew blessings, which you will be asked to commit to memory. (Don't worry about this too much. If you blank out on the words, the rabbi will prompt you.) These blessings plus three immersions in the water comprise the entire *mitzvah.*

Once you are in the water, the attendant or rabbi may ask if you are ready. When you are, duck under the water so that every strand of hair is submerged. Lift your feet off the floor and take your hands away from the sides—you'll probably be in a semi-squatting or fetal position. Eyes and lips should be neither open wide nor shut tight, rather like those of a fetus in the womb. Open your fingers and spread your toes so that the water can touch every part of you. Relax. You need only stay under for a moment or two.

When you emerge, you say the following blessing in Hebrew:

בָּרוּךְ אַתָּה יְיָ, אֱלֹהֵינוּ מֶלֶךְ הָעוֹלָם,
אֲשֶׁר קִדְּשָׁנוּ בְּמִצְוֹתָיו, וְצִוָּנוּ עַל הַטְּבִילָה.

Baruch ata Adonai Eloheynu melech ha-olam,
asher kid'shanu be-mitzvotav vitzivanu al ha-t'vilah

Blessed are You, Ruler of the Universe, Who sanctifies us with Your commandments and commands us concerning immersion.

After this blessing, immerse yourself two more times in the same loose, floating fashion. When you come up, recite the *shehehiyanu,* the blessing of thanksgiving said at special moments in life.

בָּרוּךְ אַתָּה יְיָ, אֱלֹהֵינוּ מֶלֶךְ הָעוֹלָם,
שֶׁהֶחֱיָנוּ וְקִיְּמָנוּ וְהִגִּיעָנוּ לַזְּמַן הַזֶּה.

Baruch ata Adonai Eloheynu melech ha-olam,
shehehiyanu, vekiamanu, vehigianu lazman hazeh

Blessed are You, Ruler of the Universe, You have kept us alive, and sustained us, and enabled us to reach this moment.

This is the entire liturgy. However, some rabbis add other prayers and elements to the ritual. Prior to the first immersion, for example, and in line with the traditional call for a "notification of the *mitzvot*" (*hoda'at ha'mitzvot*), the rabbi may ask a series of questions that formally affirm your decision. After the last blessing (the *shehehiyanu*) the rabbi may conclude with a few lines from the prophet Ezekiel. (See the ceremony described at the end of this chapter.) If a cantor is present, he or she may sing a short song as you rise from the water.

After you are finished in the *mikvah*, the attendant (or one of your guests/witnesses) will hand you a large towel or robe so you can return to the bathroom and dress.

PREPARING FOR *MIKVAH*: Although *mikvah* is a beautiful and spiritually powerful ritual, Jews-by-choice are sometimes dismayed by the informal, even perfunctory, atmosphere that prevails at most *mikva'ot*. In Orthodox practice (and the *mikvah* is usually an Orthodox place), the emphasis tends to be on the letter rather than the spirit of the law. The lack of decorum (much less ceremony) reflects the Orthodox view that spiritual transformation is an altogether interior event that requires little if any public acknowledgment.[26] The attendants may be brusque, people may be chatting casually in the hall-way as you enter the water, and you may even feel rushed so that the next person can get into the water.

To help you focus on the experience of *mikvah* and the step you are taking, prepare yourself by:

- Visiting the *mikvah* in advance, if possible.
- Making sure you know what's going to happen. Ask the rabbi to go over the ceremony, down to the last detail: Where will he/she and the other witnesses be standing? What happens if you blank out on the blessings? (You won't, but it's reassuring to know "what if.") Where will your fiancé be during your immersion?
- While you're showering or (better still) soaking in a bathtub, take a few minutes for deep breathing, prayer, or meditation. Bring something appropriate to read, such as one of the *kavannot* (intentional poems) at the end of this chapter.
- Bring people with you. Generally, a spouse or fiancé will accompany his or her beloved to the *mikvah*, but others may come as well. Although some people prefer to savor this moment in private, others arrive at the *mikvah* accompanied by welcoming in-laws, supportive family members, mentors, and friends from conversion class. If you wish, guests of the same sex can come into the room containing the *mikvah* while you immerse. (This is common during the conversion of children, described in a later chapter.)

- Plan the day around your *mikvah*. People tend to underestimate the power of the ritual and the need to pause and savor it. If possible, take the whole day off. Or at least schedule some time after the *mikvah* for a walk in a park or a festive meal with your partner, and/or rabbi and other guests.
- Remember that the more intention—in Hebrew, *kavannah*—you bring to your *mikvah,* the more memorable and meaningful it will be.

NATURAL ALTERNATIVES: One way to avoid the lack of spirituality or decorum of community *mikva'ot* is to do your immersion in a body of natural water. It is perfectly kosher (fit or proper) to use a pond, lake, river, or ocean—any body of flowing, nonstagnant water—for your immersion.

Choosing an outdoor setting means that your ceremony isn't dependent on the *mikvah* lady's schedule, but it does pose other kinds of logistical problems, such as weather and climate. Not all rabbis are comfortable with the idea, and in some cases it may be more difficult to convene a *bet din* at a remote lake than at the community *mikvah.* Nevertheless, those converts who have done *mikvah* out-of-doors report that immersion surrounded by a circle of trees or an ocean horizon is a peak experience.

Outdoor *mikvah* is a bit of a challenge in terms of respecting the modesty of the convert, but this is not an unsurmountable problem. You can enter the water in a bathing suit and then remove it before saying the blessings. A group of friends can walk you into the water, holding a towel around you. One woman took a small, flat-bottomed boat to the middle of a pond, disrobed under a towel, and slipped into the water. She then shouted the blessings to the rabbis who stood on the shore.

KAVANNOT: The root of *kavannah* means "direction" or "aim." *Kavannah* is also the name of a personal prayer or meditation done in preparation for a religious act. The following prayers are for reading (aloud or silently) prior to immersion, to help you focus on the choice you are undertaking, on the holiness of your actions, and on the beauty of the moment.

O God, Fountain of Life,

I enter the *mikvah* as an expression of love. I immerse myself as a sign of my faith in Israel and in the waters of Torah.

Even as our ancestors crossed the sea on their way to Sinai, may my *tevilah* be my crossing to the ways of Your law, to the sheltering wings of *Shechinah*.

May the words of my mouth, the meditations of my heart, and this act of sanctification seal my devotion to a life of Torah, *avodah,* and *gemilut hasadim;* a life of learning Your ways, a life of standing in Your presence, a life made holy by acts of loving-kindness.

Rabbi's Prayer

As you enter the living waters of the *mikvah*, I pray that you will always immerse yourself in the living waters of our tradition.

As the waters surround you with their warm embrace, know that the Jewish people embrace you and welcome you.

May the God whom we call *mikvah Yisrael*—the God Who is the source of living waters—be with you now and always.

As you enter the waters in peace, may you emerge as a source of peace and a blessing to your family, to your congregation, to the Jewish people, and to the world.

Shared Kavannah

FOR THE RABBI AND CONVERT TO SAY TO AND WITH EACH OTHER:

Today you/I begin your/my life as a Jew. As you/I enter these living waters, you/I become a part of our history that begins with creation, when the presence of God hovered over the surface of the water.

When our ancestors fled the bondage of Egypt, it was the waters of the sea that transformed a nation of slaves into a nation committed to freedom for all humankind.

Throughout the generations, water has been a symbol of a learning that sustains life. For as water brings life to the world, so does Torah bring meaning to life.

These are waters of creation, these are waters of redemption, these are waters of understanding. These are warm waters that will bring you/me beneath the sheltering wings of *Shechinah*, the loving presence of God.

Meditation Before Mikvah

It is between you and the water now
The water is the medium
Inscribing your decision
to become a Jew

You have brought yourself here
You will rise from the waters
a child of Zion

The world bows in deference to your insight
The heavens sing in your honor
In faith, Israel offers you *mikvah*
The gift of living water
Go to it as you would your next breath

Blessed is the Holy One Who witnesses the
    transformation of souls.
Blessed is the Holy One Who has chosen you for the
    people Israel.
Blessed are you who chooses the people Israel
    through the water.

FOR THE CONVERT:

It is between me and the water now
The water is my medium
With it I inscribe my name
invisible and permanent
The house of Israel becomes my home

Another step of being
a path traced with new eyes

I will open myself in the water
immerse myself whole
And I will emerge
complicated and honest as ever
A Jew

Blessed is the Holy One to whom I entrust the
     transformations of my soul.
Blessed is the Holy One Who has chosen me for the
     people Israel.
Blessed am I, who chooses the people Israel, through
     the water.

NOA RACHAEL KUSHNER

Tevilah
A Conversion Ceremony[27]

The convert enters the *mikvah* and submerges up to the neck. The rabbi then asks the following questions and the convert replies to each one:

Do you, of your own free will, choose to enter into the covenant between God and the people Israel, and to become a Jew?

Do you accept Judaism to the exclusion of all other religious faiths and practices?

Do you pledge your loyalty to the Jewish people under all circumstances?

Do you commit yourself to the pursuit of Torah and Jewish learning?

Do you promise to establish a Jewish home, and to participate in the life of the Jewish people?

If you are blessed with children, do you promise to rear them as Jews?*

The rabbi then indicates that the convert may submerge fully. Upon emerging, he/she recites the blessing:

בָּרוּךְ אַתָּה יְיָ, אֱלֹהֵינוּ מֶלֶךְ הָעוֹלָם,
אֲשֶׁר קִדְּשָׁנוּ בְּמִצְוֹתָיו, וְצִוָּנוּ עַל הַטְּבִילָה.

Baruch ata Adonai Eloheynu melech ha-olam, asher kid'shanu be-mitzvotav vitzivanu al ha-t'vilah

* *If the convert is already raising Jewish children, the last two questions are modified.*

Holy One of Blessing, Your Presence Fills Creation, You sanctify us with Your commandments and command us concerning immersion.

The convert immerses two more times and then recites the *shehehiyanu:*

בָּרוּךְ אַתָּה יְיָ, אֱלֹהֵינוּ מֶלֶךְ הָעוֹלָם,
שֶׁהֶחֱיָנוּ וְקִיְּמָנוּ וְהִגִּיעָנוּ לַזְּמַן הַזֶּה.

Baruch ata Adonai Eloheynu melech ha-olam,
shehehiyanu, vekiamanu, vehigianu lazman hazeh
Holy One of Blessing, Your Presence Fills Creation, You have kept us alive, and sustained us, and enabled us to reach this moment.

The rabbi recites:

With pure waters will I purify you, and you will be pure. A new heart will I give you, and a new spirit will I put within you. I will cause you to follow My teachings, and you shall keep My statutes. You shall be My people and I will be your God.
(Ezekiel 36:25–28)

The rabbi, *bet din,* and other witnesses greet the convert:

Welcome, brother/sister! *Mazel tov!*

After the convert has dressed, the rabbi and *bet din* join him or her to say the Shema, offer congratulations, sing a song, and sign the conversion documents.

Conversion Ceremonies

The giving of Torah happened at one specified time,
but the receiving of Torah happens all the time,
in every generation.

MEIR ALTER, THE GERER REBBE

EWISH LAW IS SATISFIED BY *MIKVAH* AND *MILAH*.
But as powerful as these rituals may be for the individual, they
provide little place for the family participation or communal
support that are central to Jewish rites of passage. Conversion
ceremonies fill those needs.

There is no standard or normative ceremony for conversion. Some are public, others private; some are simple, others
elaborate. Most share one powerful core element, however:
standing on the *bimah,* in front of family, friends, and members of the congregation, the new Jew holds the Torah and recites the Shema. The weight of the scrolls in your arms enacts
your commitment to Judaism in a tangible way and symbol-

izes a personal experience of Sinai—of receiving and choosing to accept a place in the covenant of Israel and among the people of Israel. The community, in return, shows its trust in you and its respect for you by handing you its most sacred possession.

Because communal openness to conversion is such a recent development, conversion ceremonies are not a universal feature of synagogue life. However, as the number of converts to Judaism grows, more and more congregations welcome new Jews with a communal and public welcome.

WHERE, WHEN, HOW: Conversion ceremonies were a nineteenth-century invention of Reform Judaism, which for many decades made "public affirmation" the only ritual required of converts.[28] Some of these were quite dramatic, with converts dressed all in white, walking down the long center aisle of great, cathedral-like synagogues. While that kind of pomp is a thing of the past, conversion ceremonies have moved so far into the mainstream that the rabbinical manuals of the three liberal movements each contain a conversion service.

This doesn't mean that any ceremony is set in stone. The recent vintage of this custom allows for a great deal of creativity, and the form and content of conversion ceremonies differ according to congregation, rabbi, and the preference of individual Jews-by-choice.[29] Many congregations honor new Jews by calling them up to the Torah for an *aliyah* during a regular Shabbat service. Some new Jews hold invitation-only gatherings, rather like weddings, which range from large assemblies of family and friends held on Sunday afternoon or Saturday evening, to intimate moments including only the convert, spouse, and *bet din* in a quiet sanctuary on a weekday afternoon. Some congregations honor all of those who converted during the past year on Shavuot, the holiday that celebrates the giving of the Torah and when the Book of Ruth is studied. In other synagogues, converts are welcomed in a *kabbalat ger* (welcoming the convert) service, held immediately prior to regular Friday evening worship. Some Jews-by-choice create original home-based ceremonies. The examples at the end of this chapter convey the range of services and ceremonies in use today.

Even so, conversion is a choice that some Jews-by-choice prefer to keep private. An intimate Shabbat dinner with a handful of close friends may be the most public ceremony you want. The decision is yours.

There are two basic types of public conversion ceremony. The first takes the form of an *aliyah** during the Torah reading at a Shabbat morning service. The second is a discrete service that is either introduced into a regular Shabbat or festival liturgy or scheduled as you wish. Ask your rabbi what the custom is in your congregation, and if it includes a whole service, ask to read it. Generally, rabbis are flexible about these kinds of rituals and will help you design or tailor a ceremony that is both meaningful and appropriate.

---

* Aliyah *literally means "to go up." To receive an* aliyah *in the synagogue is to be called to the Torah, and is an honor.*

ALIYAH: This is a very traditional way to link the personal and communal aspects of your new Jewishness. The custom varies from one congregation to the next, but in general, the Jew-by-choice is called up to the Torah on the Shabbat immediately following his or her *mikvah.* (If you want to postpone it until family can attend, that's usually an option, too.)

The rabbi or cantor will call you by your newly chosen Hebrew name. Depending upon synagogue custom, you may be asked to take the Torah scroll out of the ark and hold it during the Shema, and/or to recite the blessings before and after the Torah reading, and/or to read part of the Torah portion in Hebrew or in English, and/or to "dress" and return the Torah to the ark. In some congregations, the new Jew is pelted with candy as he/she returns to her seat.[30]

While you are on the *bimah,* the rabbi will introduce you to the congregation and perhaps address a few remarks to you. You may be given the opportunity to read a personal statement about becoming a Jew. In some congregations, the cantor sings or leads a song, or chants a blessing called a *mi she'beirach* for you.

מִ שֶׁבֵּרַךְ אֲבוֹתֵינוּ אַבְרָהָם יִצְחָק וְיַעֲקֹב
וְאִמּוֹתֵינוּ שָׂרָה רִבְקָה לֵאָה וְרָחֵל
הוּא יְבָרֵךְ אֶת _____
שֶׁעָלָה (עָלְתָה) הַיּוֹם לַתּוֹרָה וְנִכְנַס בְּתוֹךְ קְהִלָּתֵינוּ
וְתִתֵּן לוֹ (לָהּ) שָׁלוֹם וְנֹאמַר, אָמֵן.

May the Source of Life Who blessed all our ancestors bless ——— ben/bat ——— as he/she comes forward to Torah and joins our community and family.

139

May he/she always be worthy of us and may we always be worthy of him/her. May his/her name be honored in all the house of Israel, and may all blessings rain down upon his/her head.

Please give him/her peace.

And let us say, Amen.[31]

SERVICES: These range from additional readings and songs inserted into a regular congregational service, to freestanding, invitation-only events. While the music, prayers, rituals, and responsive readings of these ceremonies vary, the following elements are common to most:

- The traditional greeting used at all life-cycle events, *baruch ha-ba,* is invoked: "Blessed are you who come in the name of Adonai. We bless you from the house of Adonai."

- The new Jew stands before the ark and is given the Torah. The Shema is recited or sung, followed by the prayer called the *ve'ahavta.*

- The rabbi poses a series of questions, or the convert reads a declaration of commitment.

- The new Jew reads a statement about his or her journey and decision. Sometimes, a spouse, partner, or fiancé will also read a statement.

- The rabbi recites the threefold priestly benediction.

- The *shehehiyanu,* the joyful prayer of thanksgiving said upon all happy occasions, is sung.

Four very different kinds of ceremonies are included here to convey the range of contemporary practice. The first is for invited guests only; the second is part of a regular Shabbat evening service; the third ceremony takes place just before Friday night services at the synagogue; and the fourth is an informal and intimate home-based ritual, reflecting the fact that there is no need for a rabbi or for a synagogue setting.

MARK'S CEREMONY: Mark and his fiancée, Marilyn, sent invitations to forty friends and relatives, asking them to meet on a Saturday evening at the synagogue in which Marilyn had grown up.

The rabbi brought the entire group—which included Mark's mother and brothers—up onto the *bimah* and had everyone stand in a circle around Mark. Marilyn draped a *tallit*—a multicolored prayer shawl that was a gift from her family, and which was raised as their *huppah* at the wedding a few months later—around his shoulders.

The rabbi talked about the meaning of the day for Mark, and about how important it was to have so many members of his family there with him, stressing that Mark's decision was not a repudiation of his past but an affirmation of his future.

The rabbi put the Torah into Mark's arms and asked him:

Do you choose to enter the eternal covenant between God and the people Israel and to become a Jew of your own free will?

Do you accept Judaism to the exclusion of all other religious faiths and practices?

Do you pledge your loyalty to Judaism and to the Jewish people under all circumstances?

Do you promise to establish a Jewish home, and to participate actively in the life of the synagogue and of the Jewish community?

Do you commit yourself to the pursuit of Torah and Jewish knowledge?

If you should be blessed with children, do you promise to raise them as Jews? [32]

The rabbi and Mark led the group in reciting the Shema.

A friend read a poem he had written for the occasion.

The rabbi placed his hands on Mark's head and concluded with the threefold benediction:[33]

With God's blessing be kept safe always
With God's blessing see the light of the
Creator around you
With God's blessing find peace and wholeness
in this world[34]

The guests then repaired to Marilyn's family home for a party.

NORIKO'S SERVICE OF ACCEPTANCE:[35] This synagogue service is held on Friday night or Shavuot, and is sometimes used for more than one convert at a time. It begins with the singing of "Ma tovu."

Responsive reading by the rabbi and congregation:

How lovely are your tents, O Jacob, your dwelling-places, O Israel!

In love I enter Your house, O God, to worship in Your sanctuary.

I rejoice in Your house, the place where Your glory dwells.

In humility I seek blessing in the presence of God, my Maker.

To you, Eternal, I offer prayer. May this be a time of joy
    and favor.

In Your great love, O God, answer me with Your saving truth.

Blessed are you who come in the name of the Eternal;

May you find blessing out of this house of God.

Rabbi:

Our God and God of our ancestors, we thank You for many
blessings. We thank You for the gift of Torah which has ever
been to us a source of strength and guidance. Today we rejoice
as we establish a new bond of fellowship within the community
of Israel and with our heritage.

We pray for blessings upon one who comes to join the
faith and people of Israel. She accepts the Torah this day even
as our ancestors stood at Sinai in ages past, choosing Your sov-
ereignty and taking upon themselves the discipline and the joys
of our sacred legacy.

Congregation:

With openness and friendship we bless you with shalom and
welcome you to this congregation. O God of Israel, teach us to
be worthy of the heritage which is ours by birth or by choice.
May we do nothing to disgrace it. May our every deed be an expression of faith, a pledge of loyalty. May we understand and

accept our duty to continue the tasks begun by generations of our people who served in Your name, to bring light and blessing to the world.

Rabbi:

We thank you, O God, for Torah. We recall in gratitude all those of the seed of Abraham and Sarah who have been faithful to the heritage of Israel and who in different times and places have joined us of their own free will to serve You in faithfulness to Torah, in fellowship with Israel, and in service to all humanity. With joy and pride we now welcome you to the faith and people of Israel.

Song: "Hinei ma tov uma na-im"

Noriko is handed the Torah and reads:

Holding this Torah scroll, which is witness to the generations, symbol and essence of the Jewish quest, I now, in the presence of this community, publicly manifest my decision to join myself to the history, purposes, and destiny of the Jewish people.

I freely choose Judaism as my living faith and civilization.

I take the people of Israel as my own, affirming its past, celebrating its present, and building toward its future;

I affirm the oneness of the God of Israel and of all humanity whose law of love and righteousness I shall uphold and live.

Rabbi:

May you grow in dedication to Torah and the covenant of peace, truth and righteousness for which it stands.

All:

Shema Yisrael Adonai Eloheynu Adonai Echad
   Hear, Israel, Our God is One God

Song (as Torah is returned to the ark): "Etz hayim hi"

Behold, a good doctrine has been given you, My Torah. Do not forsake it. It is a tree of life to those who hold fast to it. All who cling to it find happiness. Its ways are ways of pleasantness and all its paths are peace.

Noriko reads a personal essay about the journey that led her to Judaism.

Rabbi:

By virtue of your study, your soul-searching, your immersion in the *mikvah,* and your own declaration, you have taken upon yourself the identity of a Jew. I am now privileged to confer upon you the Hebrew name which you have chosen.

As you enter the covenant of our people, we welcome you and announce your name to be Noa bat Avraham Avienu v' Sarah Imenu. May it be a name that brings blessing to Israel.

May God who blessed our ancestors, Abraham and Sarah, Isaac and Rebecca, Jacob, Leah, and Rachel, and who enabled you to reach this day, grant you blessings of life abundant. May you grow in health and strength, in wisdom and humility, in love and loyalty, in faith and moral courage, that you may bring honor to your people, goodness to the world, and be a true servant of God.

May God bless and protect you. May you feel God's presence and grace around you. May God's grace accompany you that you may find peace and be a source of peace to Israel and the world.

KABBALAT GER *FOR DAVID:* Just before Friday evening services began, the rabbi called David, the members of the *bet din,* family, friends, and anyone who was at the synagogue to come up onto the *bimah.*

Rabbi:

For 120 generations Jews have observed Shabbat. Each generation contributed something special to the holiness of the Sabbath. The mystics in sixteenth-century Safed introduced the custom of going out to the fields to welcome the Sabbath Queen as Israel's bride, giving us the service of *Kabbalat Shabbat.* Our generation introduces a new custom, too.

We come into the sanctuary just before Shabbat begins to welcome you as a member of the Jewish people. We do this for you, David, and for ourselves as well. For you, so that you will always remember your first Shabbat as a Jew. For us, so that the household of Israel may offer you welcome and take pride in your becoming a Jew.

Song: "Lecha dodi"

The rabbi opens the ark, faces David, and says:
Baruch ha-ba. Blessed are you who come in God's name.

We bless you from the house that belongs to God.

The Talmud says, If a person comes to you and desires to become a Jew, you are to say to them, "Do you not know that Jews have been harried, driven out, persecuted, and harassed, and that sufferings befall them?"

David:
Yes, I know this.

Rabbi:
These are the very words that the tradition requires. And now we ask you, David:

Do you, of your own free will, seek admittance to the Jewish people?

Have you severed all other religious affiliations?

Do you pledge your loyalty to the Jewish people amid all circumstances and conditions?

Do you promise to establish a Jewish home and to participate in the life of the synagogue and the Jewish community?

If you should be blessed with children, do you promise to rear them as Jews?

The rabbi hands David the Torah and asks him to lead the Shema:
Shema Yisrael Adonai Eloheynu Adonai Echad
Hear, Israel, Our God is One God.

A member of the *bet din* reads:
Dearer to God are the *gerim* who have come of their own ac-

cord than all the crowds of the Israelites who stood before Mount Sinai. For had the Israelites not witnessed the thunders, lightning, quaking mountain, and sounding trumpets, they would not have accepted the Torah.

But the *ger,* who saw not one of these things, came and surrendered himself to the Holy One, whose name is a blessing, and took the yoke of heaven upon himself. Can anyone be dearer to God than him? (Midrash Tanhuma)

David reads an essay statement about his decision to become a Jew and concludes with a quotation from the Book of Ruth: Wherever you go, I will go. Wherever you live, I will live. Your people shall be my people and your God my God.

The rabbi stands before the ark with David and speaks to him privately while the cantor sings "Lech lecha":

Your name in Israel from this day forth will be David Barak ben Avraham v'Sarah. May it be a name that always brings pride to the house of Israel. May the house of Israel always be a source of pride to you.

All sing *shehehiyanu* and "Siman tov u'mazel tov"

HAVDALAH *AT HOME*: Chris and Jesse had been living together in what was essentially a Jewish home for six years when Chris decided to convert. A few days after her *mikvah,* the couple invited several members of their congregation plus friends and family members to their house to celebrate *havdalah*, the ceremony on Saturday evening that separates Shabbat from the rest of the week, and which celebrates distinctions.

After lighting a new, rainbow-colored *havdalah* candle, Jesse explained that this ceremony marked a special moment of separation in Chris's life between being a non-Jew and becoming a Jew. Chris read an essay she'd written about the life journey that brought her to this moment, and concluded with the famous words from the Book of Ruth:

> Wherever you go, I will go. Wherever you live, I will live.
> Your people shall be my people and your God my God.
> Where you die, I will die and there I will be buried.

Guests were invited to offer blessings for Chris as she began her Jewish life. People took turns wishing her wise teachers, joyful holidays, a supportive community, and time for reading all the books she received as gifts on the occasion of her conversion.

After the traditional blessings over wine and spices, a final *havdalah* prayer was distributed and read by everyone present:[36]

> Holy One of Blessing, Your Presence Fills Creation
> You make the distinction between holy and not yet
> holy
> between light and darkness
> between Shabbat and the six days of the week
> between Israel and the other peoples
> between love and aloneness

between longing and belonging
between personal goals and common goals
between dreams and doing
Blessed are You Who distinguishes
between what is holy and what is not yet holy

After the light was extinguished, the company sang *shehe-hiyanu* and a festive meal was served.

Conversion of Children

THE CONVERSION OF CHILDREN USED TO BE relatively rare, but the increase in the number of adoptions, intermarriages, and stepfamilies in the Jewish community has made it an ever more common event. And while Jewish tradition does not make much of a legal or ritual distinction between the conversion of children and adults, there are real emotional and logistical differences to consider.

The fundamental difference is that children do not ask to convert, nor are they capable of making a decision of this magnitude. The choice and the responsibility rest with parents, who formally and ritually commit themselves to the task of raising their child as a Jew, which includes providing a Jewish education and teaching a Jewish identity. Parents who convert a child make an implicit promise to act as Jewish role models, to live a Jewish life themselves.

Even so, there are no guarantees that a child you have converted in infancy will embrace Judaism as an adult. The same can be said of children who are born to Jewish parents. Ultimately, all Jewish children grow up to make their own Jewish choices. If your goal is to have your child embrace Judaism, your job is to demonstrate that Judaism is an irresistible choice.

Choosing Judaism for a child raises many questions, none of which come with generic answers. Issues and solutions vary according to each child's age, health, and developmental stage, family constellation, and synagogue affiliation. While adoption is the most common reason for the conversion of children, it is by no means the only one. Intermarried couples who decide to raise their children as Jews and remarried parents who are converting and wish to convert a child face similar choices and dilemmas.

Although the particulars do matter, there are a few common "ground rules" when it comes to converting children. First, it is crucial that parents agree with each other regarding every aspect of this decision. If divorce is part of the family's history, the ex-husband or -wife must be consulted, and all of the child's grandparents deserve to be informed of plans for conversion as well. Certainly, the child deserves the fullest explanation he or she can understand, and if he/she is old and mature enough to participate in the conversation, his/her wishes must be taken into consideration.

Your rabbi will meet with you to discuss the decision and

the process of conversion, and may be helpful in explaining your choices to family members, both Jewish and non-Jewish. However, it's also a good idea to seek advice from other parents who have been down this road before you. Ask your rabbi whether there are families in your congregation who have adopted and/or converted a child, or call your local Jewish family and children's agency, which provides services for adoptive families, or contact Stars of David (described later in this chapter).

As with adult conversion, the thorny question of Jewish status arises for children, too. (See "Who Is a Jew?" in "New Definitions.") According to Jewish law, a child born to a non-Jewish mother cannot be considered Jewish even if the child lives in a Jewish home and is given a Jewish education. His/her legal status is independent of environment, affiliation, or self-concept.[37] In order for a non-Jewish child to become Jewish, *halachah* requires *mikvah*, immersion in a ritual bath, for all converts regardless of sex or age. *Brit milah,* the covenant of circumcision, or *hatafat dam brit,* a symbolic circumcision, is required of all male converts. A *bet din*—a rabbinical court—must witness the rituals.

The Conservative movement follows tradition and requires that all adoptive children go to the *mikvah* and that boys undergo *brit milah* or *hatafat dam brit.* The Reconstructionist and Reform movements accept converts without *milah* or *mikvah,* and according to the doctrine of patrilineal descent also accept the children of Jewish fathers as Jews without need of conversion; nevertheless, many individual Reconstructionist and Reform rabbis urge full ritual observance and some require it.

Even so, any conversion supervised by non-Orthodox rabbis (including conversions with *mikvah* and *milah*) will not be acceptable in all of the Orthodox community. Since the Orthodox rabbinate exercises legal control over issues of personal status in Israel, this may become an issue if your child decides to move there. Families with concerns about acceptance in Israel or challenges to the Jewishness of their child should discuss these matters with their rabbi.

THE COVENANT OF CIRCUMCISION: *Brit milah* is the oldest continuing ritual of Jewish life, one of the most joyful events in the Jewish life cycle, and the most difficult *mitzvah* asked of Jewish parents. All Jewish parents ask themselves, "Why are we doing this to our baby?" The most simple and compelling answer is that *brit milah* is such an ancient and continuous fixture of Jewish life that to stop doing it is to stop being Jews. In practice, *brit milah* is the most triumphant of Jewish celebrations, announcing to the world, "We're still here. Beginning with this baby, a new generation of Jews has arrived."

For newborns, *brit milah* for conversion is virtually indistinguishable from *brit milah* for a born-Jew. The *bris** takes place on the eighth day or, if there are health concerns, as soon as possible thereafter. Infant circumcision usually takes place in the family's home, where friends and family gather to witness and celebrate. The ceremony is performed by a *mohel,*

---

*Bris *is the Yiddish pronunciation of* brit, *and the most familiar name for the procedure and ritual. For more about planning a* bris *for an infant, see* The New Jewish Baby Book *by Anita Diamant (Jewish Lights Publishing, 1993).*

someone trained in both the rituals and procedures, though if your rabbi is present, he or she may recite some of the blessings. Afterward, a festive meal, a *s'eudat mitzvah,* is served.

If the baby was not born to a Jewish mother, tradition calls for the *bet din,* a rabbinical court of three Jews, to witness that the *bris* was performed for the purpose of conversion, which will be finalized by immersion in a *mikvah.* This is expressed in the *mohel's* prayer, which is recited immediately prior to the circumcision:

בָּרוּךְ אַתָּה יְיָ, אֱלֹהֵינוּ מֶלֶךְ הָעוֹלָם,
אֲשֶׁר קִדְּשָׁנוּ בְּמִצְוֹתָיו, וְצִוָּנוּ לָמוּל אֶת הַגֵּרִים.

Holy One of Blessing, Your Presence Fills Creation, You make us holy with Your commandments, calling us to circumcise the convert.

During the longer blessing after the circumcision, the *mohel* also says:

בָּרוּךְ אַתָּה יְיָ, אֱלֹהֵינוּ מֶלֶךְ הָעוֹלָם, אֲשֶׁר קִדְּשָׁנוּ
בְּמִצְוֹתָיו, וְצִוָּנוּ לָמוּל אֶת הַגֵּרִים וּלְהַטִּיף מֵהֶם דַּם
בְּרִית, שֶׁאִלְמָלֵא דַם בְּרִית לֹא נִתְקַיְמוּ שָׁמַיִם
וָאָרֶץ, שֶׁנֶּאֱמַר: אִם לֹא בְרִיתִי יוֹמָם וָלַיְלָה חֻקּוֹת
שָׁמַיִם וָאָרֶץ לֹא שָׂמְתִּי. בָּרוּךְ אַתָּה יְיָ, כּוֹרֵת
הַבְּרִית.

Holy One of Blessing, Your Presence Fills Creation, You make us holy with Your commandments, calling us to circumcise the convert and to draw the blood of the convert. Were it not for the blood of the covenant, heaven and earth would not have been fulfilled, as it is said, "Without My covenant, I would not set forth day and night and the laws of heaven and earth."

Holy One of Blessing, Author of the covenant.

After the circumcision itself is done, many parents personalize the ritual by reading a statement, poem, or blessing and by talking about the baby's name and namesake. Parents of adopted sons sometimes talk about how their son came to them and/or read the following prayer:

We are grateful to God
Who has made this miracle of creation
And given us this baby boy.
His coming into our home has blessed us.
He is part of our family and our lives.
This child has now become our son.
    Out of our love of God and Torah and Israel,
We wish to raise our son as a Jew.
We come now before a Jewish court of three
To begin his entry into the Jewish people
Through the *mitzvah* of *milah*.
Let this be the beginning
Of his living a life of *mitzvot*.
    May we be privileged to raise him up
As a true and loyal son of Abraham and Sarah.
This child comes into the covenant in our presence.

> We welcome him with the words that God spoke to
>> Abraham our father:
>> *Hit-halech l'fanai veh-yeh tamim*
>> Walk before Me and be whole.[38]

Circumcision for older infants and children presents more complex difficult choices. The universal advice of *mohelim*, physicians, rabbis, and adoptive parents is to have *brit milah* performed at the earliest possible date. The longer you wait, the more emotionally and physically difficult it will be both for your son and for you.

For babies under the age of three months, *brit milah* is often done in much the same way it is performed on an eight-day-old baby. For older babies, restraint is a primary concern, and while a local anesthetic will relieve pain, a safe incision requires total immobilization, which gets increasingly difficult as a baby's motor skills develop. This is why, after the baby reaches about three months of age, circumcisions are almost always done under general anesthesia, which actually poses a greater health risk than the circumcision itself. Most hospitals will not schedule elective surgery until a child is eighteen months old, or large enough to tolerate the effects of anesthesia.

At that point, a urologist, pediatrician, or surgeon performs the circumcision, and there are *mohelim* certified by the Conservative and Reform movements who are qualified in these fields. Occasionally, a Jewish physician who is not a *mohel* will do the surgery and say the blessings. If the only available qualified doctor is a non-Jew, a *mohel* (or indeed any Jew) may attend and say the blessing. If necessary, the medical circumcision can be performed without ritual and followed by *hatafat dam brit* at a later date.

As with adult circumcision, this is day surgery for a child. Your son will be released when the anesthetic has worn off. He will experience some discomfort postsurgically, but the doctor can recommend or prescribe pain medication. The wound will heal within a week, though discoloration may last some time longer.

Putting an older, self-conscious boy through the rigors of surgery on his penis is bound to be confusing at best, terrifying and traumatic at worst. Even so, many rabbis and parents feel that circumcision is ultimately nonnegotiable. As the adoptive mother of two sons explains it, "We considered letting the boys grow up and make the decision for themselves. It would have been an easier way out for us as parents." But ultimately, she and her husband went ahead with the procedure. "I could only say to them that if I did not have them circumcised, I would not be treating them like my true sons . . . the same as if they had been born to me as babies."[39]

However, some parents who adopt older sons forgo circumcision or postpone it indefinitely. Since virtually all male Jews are circumcised, this is a controversial choice. And while most rabbis encourage *brit milah,* there have always been exceptions: the Talmud excused sons known to be hemophiliacs. One *mohel* argues that since the biblical commandment is for *brit milah* on the eighth day, if a boy was not your son on the eighth day—or even in the eighth month, or the eighth year—the rule does not fully apply to parents who adopt an older boy.[40]

These arguments cannot erase the physical difference between a noncircumcised boy and other Jewish men. By the time of his bar mitzvah, the age at which converted children have the legal right to renounce their Jewishness (explained later in this chapter), you and the rabbi might want to discuss the subject of circumcision and formal conversion with your son, presenting them as choices for him to consider. It may help to reassure him that his situation is not unique; like many uncircumcised Russian Jews who embraced their Jewish birthright after immigrating to the United States or Israel, your son can think of himself as a Jew in need of a circumcision.

RITUAL CIRCUMCISION: If a boy was circumcised without religious ceremony, the ritual of *hatafat dam brit* is performed by a *mohel*, who numbs the penis with an anesthetic spray, draws a drop of blood from the site of the circumcision, and recites the blessing for circumcising the convert. (See the discussion on *hatafat dam brit* in the chapter "The Covenant of Circumcision.")

Although this ritual is certainly far less traumatic than circumcision, it, too, should be scheduled at the earliest possible date. While the pain is minimal, the prospect is bound to be frightening. If your son is old enough to understand what's going to happen to him, explain the procedure as matter-of-factly as you can. If you let your child see that you are anxious or upset about this, he will be, too.

This symbolic circumcision is generally done simply, quickly, and without ceremony, although some *mohelim* do add the blessing for circumcising the convert. It can take place in a doctor's office, in your home, or sometimes in the waiting room of the *mikvah* immediately before immersion. When it's all over with, you can add a *shehehiyanu*, the prayer of thanksgiving for new blessings, and *kiddush*, the blessing over wine, to add a festive note.

In order for the conversion of males to be complete, they must also be immersed in a *mikvah*. There is no need for the two rituals to occur on the same day.

MIKVAH: Although all converts to Judaism are required to undergo immersion in a ritual bath, dunking a child under-water—especially a child who is too young to swim—makes most parents understandably anxious. There is no need to panic; no one has ever drowned in a *mikvah*, and indeed, few babies even object. The secret is to blow directly into the child's face; she will reflexively close her eyes and hold her breath for the instant it takes to duck her under. Rabbis and cantors with years of experience swear this trick never fails, and parents who follow their advice are amazed at how well it works.

The success of the "blow-and-duck" trick argues in favor of taking children to the *mikvah* at the earliest possible date. For children who are old enough to understand that they will be going for a "dip," tell them what's going to happen. Do not hide or lie about the fact that the head has to go underwater, too. If your child is afraid of the water or terrified about putting her face under the surface, consider postponing your trip to the *mikvah* until she is comfortable in water. It's better to wait until your child says she's ready than to hear her screams echoing off the tiled walls.

Whenever you feel your child is ready, start talking about the *mikvah* a few weeks before the event is scheduled. Describe what the *mikvah* looks like, what will happen there, and who will be there with you. Reassure your child that you will be in the water with him or her every second. Indeed, one or both parents (usually wearing bathing suits) will take the child into the water.

Rehearse what will happen in the *mikvah* in the bathtub or at a swimming pool. Encourage your child to duck under the surface and teach her to make bubbles underwater. Practice being fish together.

Ask the attendant to give you a tour of the building before you begin to prepare for your immersion; the response will depend upon the schedule and the attendant's attitude, but it's certainly worth asking.

Older children can be reassured that their modesty will be scrupulously protected; even though converts must enter the waters of the *mikvah* completely nude, the only person who sees them in the water (to check that they have immersed completely) will be someone of the same sex. The *bet din* does not have to see the immersion, and rarely asks them questions. Parents usually say the two blessings for immersion. (See the chapter "*Mikvah*: A River from Eden.")

Your child's *mikvah* will, in all likelihood, be a powerful and moving experience for you. But don't expect it to mean as much to your child, especially if he is under the age of eight.

While he may find it a kind of adventure, children rarely understand the religious significance of what seems like a trip to a miniature indoor swimming pool.

Even so, you can make this into a positive experience and a happy memory for children. Take pictures outside the *mikvah* (before and after) and at the signing of certificates. Make sure there are familiar faces inside or just outside the *mikvah*. Ask the rabbi or cantor to add a Hebrew song that your child knows. And make the immersion just the beginning of a celebration. Bring friends to be witnesses, to toss confetti in the parking lot, and to accompany you home for cake and ice cream. Or follow up your trip to the *mikvah* with a visit to a Jewish bookstore for a new book or tape or toy of your child's choice. Some parents give their children a necklace—a *mezuzah* or Star of David—in honor of the occasion. As the years go by, your child will pore over the photographs and ask to hear the story about the day he or she became a Jew.

NAMING A CONVERTED CHILD: American Jews tend to follow the same custom in naming their sons and daughters whether children were born to them or adopted. Thus, most parents give children English and/or Hebrew names in memory of family members who have died, creating a living link with previous generations of Jews. Naming your daughter Rachel in honor of your grandmother connects her to everyone in her family who still remembers Grandma Rachel, and to those who are no longer here to remember. It also connects her to the Rachel of the Torah, and to all the Jewish women who were named Rachel who lived before her, and to all the Rachels yet to come.[41]

Unlike adult converts, who usually take the name of Abraham and Sarah as their spiritual parents (see the chapter "Choosing a Hebrew Name"), children are usually known by their Jewish parents' names. Thus, an adopted Rachel will be called to the Torah as Rachel bat Shimon v'Penina, or Rachel the daughter of Simon and Pearl. Likewise, a converted Aaron would be known as Aharon ben Yacov v'Malkah, or Aaron the son of Jack and Molly.[42]

Children's names are often bestowed in public ceremonies. Traditionally, boys are named at their *brit milah* and girls are named in the synagogue or at a home-based ceremony. In some synagogues, adoptive families are called to the Torah, where the rabbi introduces the child to the entire community by announcing his or her Hebrew name.

In cases where an adopted child already had a given name, parents have a variety of choices. If the child is an infant, some parents drop the name given by the birth parents or orphanage entirely. But other adoptive parents add a first name and use the birth name as a middle name. Thus, a baby adopted from Korea might be named Rebecca Seong.[43]

ADOPTION: Adopting a child is a great joy often arrived at after great pain. For many people, adoption is a last resort that follows years of infertility treatments, pregnancy losses, and the searing realization that a biological child is an impossibility. Following that blow comes the sometimes lengthy, frustrating process of adoption. Then, after years of emotional stress and strain, Jewish adoptive parents face the additional complication of conversion.

Children—whether born to you or adopted—confront parents with ultimate questions. For most people, the miracle of being given a child to raise is a revelation about the sanctity of life. For Jews, regardless of how unaffiliated or nonobservant, parenthood often summons up surprisingly deep feelings and assumptions about Judaism. Staring into the face of your baby, overwhelmed by feelings of love, gratitude, and fear ("Now what do I do?"), you may find yourself facing a host of difficult questions about Jewish identity, status, authenticity, and belonging:

How could this towheaded baby possibly "look Jewish"? What right have I to choose a religious identity for a child who was born into another faith or culture? How will I react if my child someday declares herself to be "part Christian" and thus entitled to a Christmas tree?

Unfortunately, too many adoptive parents struggle with these kinds of questions in isolation. Jews tend to affiliate with synagogues and other Jewish institutions when their children begin school, which means they know nothing about the ethnic diversity in a given synagogue's preschool, or that Jewish families now come in all shapes, all sizes, and a rainbow of colors. Support and practical information are available if you seek out other Jewish adoptive parents and adoption professionals. Call your local Jewish family and children's organization to see whether they offer adoption services. Speak with rabbis or education directors at area synagogues, who can refer you to other adoptive parents in their congregations. Contact Stars of David, a nonprofit, national support network for Jewish adoptive parents.

Founded in 1984, Stars of David has active chapters in cities around the country, and a membership that includes Jews of all affiliations, intermarried couples, single parents, prospective parents, interracial couples with biological children, and grandparents. Chapters are linked by a national newsletter called *Star Tracks*.*

The history of Jewish adoption and conversion has deep roots but is not widely known. Pharoah's daughter, Moses' adoptive mother, was the subject of rabbinic accolades in the Talmud, and certainly Jews have always considered it a *mitzvah* to take in orphaned children. According to Jewish law, foster or adoptive parents assume all the responsibilities of biological parents, and the rabbis tended to favor "nurture" over "nature." The Talmud states, "Those who raise a child are called its parents, and not the ones who conceived it."[44]

During the Second Commonwealth (538 B.C.E.–70 C.E.), Jews were known for their practice of rescuing gentile children who were orphaned or outcast and rearing them as Jews.[45] But that was before Christian and Muslim laws made converting to Judaism a capital crime, and since then Judaism concerned itself, for the most part, with the needs of orphans born to Jewish parents.†

Today, nearly all children adopted by Jews were born to non-Jewish parents. While this was the exception in the past,

---

* *See Resources.*
† *See Part VI, "Your History: A Short History of Conversion to Judaism."*

it did occur often enough that Jewish law responded by making the conversion of minors provisional until a child reached maturity. When a child reared as a Jew but born to a non-Jewish mother reaches the age of religious adulthood (traditionally, thirteen for boys and twelve for girls), he or she is given the right to affirm or renounce his or her Jewishness. There is no drama or ceremony connected with this "right." An adult who knows of his or her origins and makes no reference to it is considered to have accepted the decision, and the conversion is finalized. However, this rule clearly mandates full disclosure of a child's adoptive status since if it is kept secret, the adoptee cannot make the decision that settles his or her Jewish status once and for all.[46]

Given the right of renunciation, some parents delay *mikvah* until just prior to bar or bat mitzvah. This formalizes and finalizes conversion and acknowledges the young person's status as a full member of the community—someone who is old enough to make this extremely important decision. However, this is a controversial choice. Waiting until adolescence lays a heavy burden upon a child at a very vulnerable stage of development. This is a time when many adopted children wrestle with the ambiguities of their identity, and the last thing they may need is another challenge: "What do you mean, I'm not *really* Jewish?"

Adolescence is rarely an easy time for parents or for teenagers. And the transitional period from childhood to adulthood may be even more complicated if your child was adopted. Since all kids tend to differentiate themselves in the struggle to define themselves, adopted Jewish teens have been known to say, "I don't have to go to Hebrew school [or cele-brate my bat mitzvah] because I'm not really Jewish anyway."

Of course, biological children sometimes make similar, equally painful statements: "I didn't decide to be Jewish; I was just born into this accidentally and you can't make me be something I don't want to be."

Adopted or biological, all teenagers deliver the same message to their parents: "I am not like you." And yet, most teenagers ultimately become adults who make choices that are remarkably similar to the ones their parents made. There are no guarantees, but if you live a Jewish life and love being Jew-ish, your example becomes an indelible part of your children's identity. After that, the choice belongs to your children, re-gardless of how they came into your life.

ADOPTION CEREMONIES: After your child has been through *mikvah* and/or *milah*, he or she is a Jew. But since those ritu-als don't express the special joy, gratitude, and awe that adop-tive parents feel, some people celebrate the adoption itself with a separate ceremony.

There is no precedent for adoption ceremonies, which means that their timing, location, and content are entirely de-termined by parents, often with assistance from a rabbi. How-ever, given the increase in adoption in the Jewish community, there is no need to reinvent the whole genre.

Most adoption ceremonies share certain core elements, such as the welcoming of the baby (*baruch ha-ba*), *shehehiyanu*, the threefold blessing, the giving of a Hebrew name, and per-sonal stories about the name. You can also include readings

Brit Imuts

Covenant of Adoption[48]

The baby is carried into the room by one grandparent and handed to the others. The parents explain the nature of the ceremony and tell the story of the baby's name.

The baby is placed on the knees of his adoptive parents, who say:

We solemnly swear, by the One Who is called loving and merciful, that we will raise this child as our own. We will nurture him/her, sustain him/her, and guide him/her in the paths of Torah, in accordance with the duties incumbent upon Jewish parents. May God ever be with him/her. We pray for the wisdom and strength to help our child, ———, become a man/woman of integrity and kindness.

FOR A BOY:
May the One Who saved us from evil bless this boy, and let him be called by our name and the names of our ancestors and may he multiply throughout the land.

FOR A GIRL:
Be blessed of the Lord, daughter, and have no fear.
I will do on your behalf whatever you ask. For you
will be a fine woman.[49]

THREEFOLD BLESSING:

יְבָרֶכְךָ יְיָ וְיִשְׁמְרֶךָ,

יָאֵר יְיָ פָּנָיו אֵלֶיךָ וִיחֻנֶּךָּ,

יִשָּׂא יְיָ פָּנָיו אֵלֶיךָ וְיָשֵׂם לְךָ שָׁלוֹם.

May God bless you and keep you. May God be
with you and gracious to you. May God show you
kindness and give you peace.

    The child is showered with wishes and bless-
ings from family and friends.
    Shehehiyanu is sung.
    Kiddush is recited, and a celebratory meal is
served.

from the Torah, blessings from guests, and a prayer for the baby's birth family. Some parents add a symbolic gesture such as washing the baby's feet or wrapping the baby in a prayer shawl as a way of enacting a child's entry into the community of Israel. A good resource for planning an adoption ceremony is *Designing Rituals of Adoption: For the Religious and Secular Community* by Mary Martin Mason (Resources for Adoptive Parents, 1995).[47]

The ceremony on pages 168–69, which has been adapted and amended many times, is an example of an adoption ceremony based on the idea of *brit*, or covenant, which is at the heart of the relationship between the Jewish people and God.

PART IV

Celebrating

Conversion

*I*s there such a thing as a "conversion party"?

*W*hat do I tell people who ask me what I'd like as a gift?

*A*re there ways to personalize the ceremonies and celebration?

*C*an we serve Chinese food (which would include my family's tradition) at the wedding reception?

*A*fter I convert, should my wife and I renew our vows in a Jewish ceremony?

*J*EWISH LIFE-CYCLE EVENTS ARE RENOWNED for the gusto with which they are celebrated. But partying is not just one of the delights of Jewish culture, it is a religious obligation. A *s'eudat mitzvah* is a commanded meal, a required part of most Jewish life-cycle events, including weddings, bar and bat mitzvahs, and following the completion of a course of study. The food and drink and conversation at such celebrations are not considered separate from the *mitzvah* itself. Indeed, the *s'eudah* blurs the line between holy and profane. The generic word for this kind of celebration is *simcha*, which means both "rejoicing" and "party."

Until recently, conversion rarely inspired *simcha*s deserving of the name. Today, however, the occasion of becoming a Jew is greeted and embraced with a wide array of joyful celebrations. Celebrating the occasion of your conversion to Judaism is a way to share your happiness with those you love.

Conversion Celebrations

Siman tov u'mazel tov
(Good luck and good fortune)

TRADITIONAL SONG

THERE ARE MANY WAYS TO CELEBRATE CONVER-
sion to Judaism. Some Jews-by-choice prefer to celebrate the
occasion of their conversion with an intimate Friday night Shabbat dinner. Others mail out invitations (ah, the wonders of desk-
top publishing), call a caterer, and invite a houseful of guests.

Because conversion used to be relatively rare, private, and
for centuries discreet, there is very little custom or Jewish
law pertaining to conversion celebrations. The lack of history
gives you the freedom to do what suits you, but it also means
that it may not even occur to your Jewish family and friends to
help you rejoice. Even your rabbi may still be unfamiliar with
the idea of associating *s'eudat mitzvah* with conversion.[1]

Although you can certainly throw your own *simcha,* it is

more appropriate for parties and receptions to be hosted by your Jewish family, friends, and members of your congregation. In other words, it might be a good idea to show this chapter to someone who loves you and supports your decision to become a Jew.

In general, *simcha*s for conversion tend to be informal gatherings where congratulations are offered and gifts are given. Usually, the new Jew is asked to say a few words about his or her decision and feelings. Sometimes, guests will offer toasts or even *d'rashot,* commentaries relevant to the convert's life, his or her Hebrew name, or how the week's Torah portion relates to the happy occasion.

It's not always easy to carve out the time or energy for a separate *simcha,* especially since so many conversions are timed to coincide with other party-intensive life-cycle events, such as your wedding or a child's bar or bat mitzvah. However, Jewish tradition emphasizes the idea that every *simcha* deserves to be celebrated and savored individually. There's even a traditional maxim to that effect: "One should not mix rejoicing with rejoicing." Your conversion deserves its own festive moment in the sun. Whenever or however you celebrate, try to time it as close to the day of your *mikvah* as possible so the experience is still fresh.

There are many ways to celebrate your conversion to Judaism:

- After your *mikvah* ceremony, go out for lunch or dinner with your beloved and/or with a whole group of friends and family.

- Plan a special dinner or luncheon at home on the Shabbat following your conversion.

- If the conversion ceremony is part of a regular worship service, let the *simcha* flow directly from the sanctuary into the social hall. Your family and friends can help host an *oneg Shabbat* (literally, "joy of the Sabbath"), the coffee hour that follows Friday evening services, or sponsor the Shabbat morning *kiddush*, a light meal that begins with blessings for wine and challah. Informal receptions such as these give members of the community a chance to welcome you personally and give you the opportunity to meet some of your new extended Jewish family. (In some congregations, the Outreach or Keruv committee takes care of this.)

- Get a guest book and ask friends to record their thoughts and wishes for the new Jew.

- Ask guests to bring a favorite Jewish recipe and create a personalized cookbook.

- At some point during the party, play some lively klezmer music and lift the new Jew on a chair like a bride or groom at a wedding.

- If your parents are supportive of your decision to convert, invite them to the celebration. Make them feel welcome and honored by including music and food that reflect their ethnic traditions as well. However, do not insist that family members attend any event that will make them unhappy or uncomfortable.

- When planning the food for your party, give some thought to *kashrut,* the laws that govern what and how Jews eat. Even if you aren't planning to keep a kosher home, providing a meal that conforms at least to the fundamentals of *kashrut* (i.e., no pork or shellfish, no milk with meat) will enable those who do observe the dietary laws to enjoy themselves. It also announces your intention to honor Jewish tradition.

- Donate three percent of the cost of the meal to Mazon: A Jewish Response to Hunger.[2] Let people at your party know of the contribution to Mazon or any other charity of your choice so that they might be inspired to do the same. (See the chapter *"Tzedakah."*)

GIFTS: Gifts are inevitable. If you have a party, people will want to bring presents. Even if you ask them not to. Even if you ask that they give money to *tzedakah* instead. Rather than fight the generous impulses of friends, you can make the party a kind of Jewish "shower" of material goods many born-Jews have been given or collected since childhood.

Books are the most common gifts given to converts, and some congregations make a practice of giving a Tanach (the book form of the Bible) to new Jews. A stack of books is a great dowry for someone with a relatively new Jewish home library; you could even go to a Jewish bookstore and "register."

There's no reason for gift books to be limited to serious religious tomes. If the new Jew is, for example, a fiction lover, the host can ask every guest to bring a favorite Jewish novel.

Cooks will welcome cookbooks, and most people are happy to receive humor books.

Subscriptions to Jewish newspapers or magazines also make excellent presents—and so do Hebrew language games and toys geared for teaching young children the *alef-bet*. A generous family member might consider giving the *Encyclopaedia Judaica*, the sixteen-volume "Britannica" of Judaism.

Ritual items are also very popular conversion gifts. These often become instant heirlooms, and anything handmade or personalized is particularly meaningful. Brides and grooms often give each other a *tallit* (prayer shawl). Other ritual gift items include: a *kiddush* cup, Shabbat candlesticks and table linen, a challah cover, seder plate, *tzedakah* box, *mezuzot* for doorways, *shofar*, and *tefillin* (phylacteries, leather boxes worn during prayer). *Kippot* (yarmulkes) are available in an endless array, from elaborately embroidered Yemenite caps to leather beanies emblazoned with the insignia of major league baseball teams. Religious jewelry—especially necklaces hung with a *mezuzah* or *magen David* (Star of David)—are perennial favorites.

For musicians and music lovers, the discography of Jewish music runs the gamut from Leonard Bernstein's *Kaddish* to klezmer, from vintage cantorial solos to the song parodies of Allan Sherman. The list goes on and on.

Other gift ideas:

• A work of Jewish art
• Tickets to a Jewish play or concert

- Paid attendance at a Jewish retreat, workshop, or class
- A year's supply of bagels
- A gift certificate to a kosher butcher
- Synagogue membership for a year
- A trip to Israel

Tzedakah

*Tzedakah is as important as all the other
commandments put together.*

BABA BATHRA 9A

WHEN YOU BECOME A JEW, *TZEDAKAH* BECOMES
your obligation and your privilege. Although the word is often
translated as "charity," *tzedakah* is based on an entirely different concept. Unlike "charity," from the Latin *caritas*, which
means Christian love, *tzedakah* is derived from the Hebrew
word *tzedek*, which means "justice."

For Jews, giving to the poor is not something you do out
of the goodness of your heart. *Tzedakah* is a *mitzvah*—a category of action that is both holy obligation and honor. But while
tzedakah is a legal duty, it is also considered a great joy. The
Zohar, the classic text of Jewish mysticism, refers to *tzedakah*
as "a tree of life."[3] Giving to others is seen as being so fundamental to human dignity that even the poor are commanded

to give to those less fortunate than themselves, even if their gift comes from *tzedakah* given to them by someone else.[4]

The long-standing tradition of giving *tzedakah* on the occasion of a personal milestone is tailor-made for your first "official" *mitzvah* as a Jew. It also finds an echo in the ancient Jewish past. According to the Talmud, circumcision and immersion were only two of three required acts for converts; the third was an "offering."[5] While the Temple in Jerusalem was standing, proselytes had to bring a sacrifice—a burnt offering of cattle or pigeons. With the destruction of the Temple in the year 70 C.E., animal sacrifice ceased and the law was abrogated. And yet, giving something tangible to the community still seems an appropriate gesture of affiliation and membership.

There are many ways to give *tzedakah*. Writing a check to any worthy charitable organization fulfills the *mitzvah*. While a gift to a Jewish charity is especially fitting at this moment in your life ("If I am not for myself, who will be?"[6]), the tradition is also clear on the point that "a Jew should give charity to a poor non-Jew."[7]

Here are some ideas that may add meaning to giving *tzedakah* as you begin your Jewish life:

- If you have a party or go out to dinner to celebrate your conversion, consider giving three percent of the cost of the meal to Mazon: A Jewish Response to Hunger. Mazon asks American Jews to contribute three percent of the cost of all life-cycle celebrations (births, weddings, bar and bat mitzvahs) to help feed the hungry. Money supports soup kitchens, food pantries, and the like, which serve both Jews and non-Jews. (Mazon, 12401 Wilshire Boulevard, Suite 303, Los Angeles, CA 90025-1015.)

• There are literally hundreds of local, national, and international Jewish organizations that need your support. Do some research and find a group that is doing work that speaks to your own concerns, interests, and point of view.

• Consider making a donation to your synagogue's library fund, or to your rabbi's discretionary fund, which is money that he or she may distribute to congregants in need or to other worthy causes.

• If there is a party to celebrate your conversion, ask that guests either refrain from buying you a gift and/or instead make a donation to either a specified organization or to their own favorite charity.

• Traditionally, the arrival of a new life in the house of Israel prompts friends and family members to have a tree planted in the land of Israel. To arrange for that honor, call the Jewish National Fund: 800-542-TREE.

• The reason Jews make contributions of $18 or multiples of the number 18 is because the numerical value of the Hebrew letters that spell out *chai*, "life," add up to 18.

• If your family has traditionally sent money to a particular charity (for example, the American Cancer Society, in memory of a loved one), a gift to that cause honors the continuity of values and commitments that have always been important to you.

Occasions for Giving Tzedakah

On the conversion of a friend

In honor of a birth, bar mitzvah, bat mitzvah,
wedding

In honor of your graduation, your spouse's new job,
your child's first day in kindergarten

In memory of someone who has died

Before candle-lighting on Friday night

Before any Jewish holiday

Upon arriving safely in Israel

Upon inheriting a sum of money or receiving a
foundation grant

In honor of someone who has reached a significant
birthday

In honor of friends hanging a *mezuzah* in their
new home

On the anniversary of your own conversion

DANNY SIEGEL (*adapted*)[8]

Hiddur Mitzvah: Making It Beautiful

According to the rabbinic principle of *hiddur mitzvah*, when a physical object is needed to fulfill a commandment, the object should be as beautiful as possible. In other words, although it is perfectly kosher to use a paper cup for *kiddush*—the blessing made over wine—it is preferable and praiseworthy to use a handsome goblet made especially for religious purposes. The same principle applies to all aspects and elements of Jewish practice. Paying attention to the details of all conversion ceremonies—through objects, music, and language—is a way of sanctifying the process.

OBJECTS: Although conversion does not require much in the way of material objects, there are a few items that, with a little forethought, can become family heirlooms. For example, the prayer shawl you wear the first time you are called to the Torah as a Jew can become a family treasure that recalls the formal beginning of your Jewish life.

There are several other ways to enhance the beauty of your conversion:

Flowers on the *bimah* during a synagogue conversion ceremony and on the tables at the *simcha* are a nice touch. (Donating them to a hospital or nursing home after the occasion spreads your happiness with an act of *tzedakah*.)

A thoughtful friend might bring you a bouquet of flowers when you leave the *mikvah*. Another way to add beauty and warmth to *mikvah* is for attendants to bring large, fluffy new bath sheets (pure white or rainbow-colored) in which to wrap the new Jew as he or she steps out of the water.

Men undergoing *hatafat dam brit* can bring a *kiddush* cup to the doctor's office or synagogue or wherever the ritual takes place. If you don't already have a special cup to use for reciting the blessing over wine, consider getting one for the occasion.

Candlelight is a universal symbol of God's presence, and candles are used at many Jewish life-cycle events, including *brit milah* and weddings. Lighting a candle at a conversion ceremony is a way for the new Jew to signal that a new soul has been added to the family of Israel. In the words of the Baal Shem Tov, "From every human being, there rises a light that reaches straight to heaven." Conversion ceremonies that coincide with *havdalah* include the many-wicked braided candle, which is available in a rainbow of colors as well as the traditional blue and white.

MUSIC: Music and song are traditional at all joyful Jewish celebrations. For many people, music is a primary source of spiritual inspiration, and nothing binds a community together better than singing.

After any conversion ritual or ceremony, your rabbi or cantor may lead a rousing chorus of "Siman tov u'mazel tov" (Good luck and good fortune). This all-purpose song of rejoicing proclaims the event a source of joy for everyone gathered and for the whole house of Israel.

Beyond that, creative cantors and musical rabbis use song both at the *mikvah* and in the synagogue to add beauty and meaning to conversion rituals.[9] At the *mikvah,* any musical setting of the *shehehiyanu* is appropriate, as are many of Debbie Friedman's songs, such as "Sing unto God" and "The promise."

Cantorial solos that suit a synagogue conversion ceremony include: "Entreat me not" by Lawrence Avery, "Song of Ruth" by Maurice Goldman, settings of "L'dor va dor" by Meir Finkelstein or by Sol Zim, "May God inspire" by Myrna Cohen, "May you live to see your world fulfilled" by Benjie Ellen Schiller and "V'erastich li" by Ben Steinberg.

Songs that work well for congregational singing include: "Lechi lach" by Debbie Friedman, "Ashreinu" by Sidney Hodkinson, "Adonai oz" by Jeff Klepper, and any setting of "Y'varechecha."[10]

WORDS: You may be asked to write an essay about your journey to Judaism, and perhaps to read it at a conversion ceremony. No matter what you write or how brief it is, this is an important document that deserves to be lovingly preserved. Your children and their children will treasure it.

Sometimes, it's hard to find words beautiful and strong enough to describe your feelings. The translations, blessings, and poems on the following pages are offered to inspire you and as readings for conversion rituals, ceremonies, or celebrations.

A Blessing

Berachot 17a
Eruvin 54a

May your eyes sparkle with the light of Torah,
and your ears hear the music of its words.
May the space between each letter of the scrolls
bring warmth and comfort to your soul.
May the syllables draw holiness from your heart,
and may this holiness be gentle and soothing
to you and all God's creatures.
May your study be passionate,
and meanings bear more meanings
until Life itself arrays itself before you
as a dazzling wedding feast.
And may your conversation,
even of the commonplace,
be a blessing to all who listen to your words
and see the Torah glowing on your face.

DANNY SIEGEL[11]

Sh'ma

Sh'ma Yisra'el Adonai Eloheynu Adonai Echad
Hear, Israel, you are of God and God is one
Baruch shem kevod malchuto le-olam va-ed
Praise the name that speaks to us through all time.

So you shall love what is holy
with all your courage, with all your passion, with all
    your strength.
Let the words that have come down
shine in our words and our actions.
We must teach our children to know and understand
    them.
We must speak about what is good and holy within
    our homes,
when we are working, when we are at play,
when we lie down and when we get up.
Let the word of your hands speak them,
let your eyes shine and see with their knowledge.
Let them run in your blood
and glow from your doors and windows.
We should love ourselves, for we are of God.
We should love our neighbors as ourselves.
We should love the stranger, for we were once
    strangers in the land of Egypt
and have been strangers in all the lands of the world
    since.
Let love fill our hearts with its clear precious water
for all living with whom we share the water of life.

Heaven and earth observe how we cherish or spoil
our world.
Heaven and earth watch whether we choose life or
choose death.
We must choose life so that we and our children's
children may live.
We must love the source of being and the power
of life.
Be quiet and listen to the still small voice within that
speaks in love.
Open to it, hear it, heed it and work for life.
Let us remember and strive to be good.
Let us remember to find what is holy
within and without.

MARGE PIERCY[12]

Israel, hear that God is one.
Blessed is the name of God's radiant presence forever.

Love God with everything you have: your heart, your
soul, your strength. These words which I give you
here and now, take them to your heart. Teach them
to those who follow you. Speak of them often: at
home, at work, and on the road; at the beginning
of your day and at its end. Hold them like a sacred
chant that whispers inside you, spilling out into song.
Feel the words in your fingertips, keep them at the
front of your mind, in the small space above your
eyes. Let them guide your vision to rest in new
places; let them soothe and disturb you. Look up
occasionally, the words will appear everywhere in the
place you call your home.

JANET BERKENFIELD[13]

Statement by a Woman Who Has Chosen to Be a Jew

I began this journey because I loved one Jew.
I sometimes imagine that, at least at first,
our ancestor Sarah might have done the same,
following her man from Haran to Canaan
through all the hardships and terrors of ancient travel
because she loved him no matter what his ideas
    or voices
or perhaps precisely *because of* his ideas and voices.
Now that is no longer good enough for me.
Now I love not only the man I chose to marry
but also the Jewish People, my People.
Where they go, I will go,
and if that means estrangement and exile,
I choose to be the stranger and the exile with them.

I have left my family to be at one with you.
I would not lie at this most awesome moment
saying it is, has been, or will be easy.
Whether they understand or not is not irrelevant,
for they bore me and raised me,
wished only the best for me, and loved me.
They are my parents.
Whether or not they stand by me
as I assume my Judaism—
they will always deserve my love in return.

But *you* must stand by me, *you*, my People,
for you have known the heart of the outcast.

I have been warned:
when the hate of Jews appears in any of its many
      faces,
each one uglier than the next,
and when it roars and growls in its most grotesque
      voice,
I know:
the curses and stares,
the primitive arrows of old
and the most modern and sophisticated weapons of
      destruction
are aimed at me.
I cannot hide anymore.

Today I cease to be safe,
as I once was in my other life.
Wherever you are shut out, I am shut out,
and I accept that
as much as I accept all promised joy
that comes to me as a Jew.

If—sitting across the room at some dinner
to raise funds for threatened Jews—

you see this face,
so different from those all around me
because of my Irish grandparents,
I am not a guest or mere sympathizer.
I *belong* there.
Your tragedies of old and of today are mine;
I take them as I take the Simchas:
the Land of Israel, Mitzvahs, Shabbat in all its glory,
food no longer permitted
now that I have walked ever so proudly over the line.

This week in the Sukkah,
I will revel in God's care,
remembering how fragile our defense is
against the mighty winds and threatening storms
that often frighten us.

I take the name Ruth as mine.
On this most meaningful day, you are my Naomi.
May I and my children be worthy parents
of the Redeemer of Israel.

Amen.

DANNY SIEGEL[14]

Why I Am a Jew

I am a Jew because the faith of Israel demands of me
no abdication of the mind.

I am a Jew because the faith of Israel requires of me
all the devotion of my heart.

I am a Jew because in every place where suffering
weeps, the Jew weeps.

I am a Jew because at every time when despair cries
out, the Jew hopes.

I am a Jew because the word of Israel is the oldest
and the newest.

I am a Jew because, for Israel, the world is not
completed: we are completing it.

I am a Jew because, for Israel, humanity is not
created: we are creating it.

I am a Jew because Israel places humanity and its
unity above the nations and above Israel itself.

I am a Jew because, above humanity, image of the
divine Unity, Israel places the unity which is
divine.

EDMUND FLEGG[15]

Rachel

For her blood runs in my blood
and her voice sings in me.
Rachel, who pastured the flocks of Laban,
Rachel, the mother of the mother.

And that is why the house is narrow for me,
and the city foreign,
for her veil used to flutter
in the desert wind.

And that is why I hold to my way
with such certainty,
for memories are preserved in my feet
ever since, ever since.

RACHEL (BLUWSTEIN)
(translated from the Hebrew by Naomi Nir)[16]

Above All,
Teach This Newborn Child

Above all, teach this newborn child to touch,
to never stop,
to feel how fur is other than the leaf or cheek,
to know through these hands diamond from glass,
Mezuzah from anything else in the world,
the same with Challah and a book.

As the baby grows,
teach this child to embrace the shoulders of another
before sadness brings them inhumanly low,
to stroke the hair softly of one younger who is
        weeping,
one older who cries.

Let these hands be a gentle Yes
when Yes is the truth
and, gently, a No when No is right.

Whatever these fingers touch—
may they be for new holiness and blessing,
for light, life, and love.

Amen.

DANNY SIEGEL[17]

A Word About Weddings

The voice of joy, the voice of gladness, the voice of the bridegroom, the voice of the bride

FROM THE SEVEN WEDDING BLESSINGS

*M*ANY CONVERSIONS TAKE PLACE WITHIN months or weeks of a new Jew's marriage to a born-Jew. While a conversion and a wedding are separate *mitzvot* and each one deserves its own honors and celebrations, the connection between them is undeniable.

There is nothing in the liturgy to distinguish a wedding between two born-Jews from a wedding where the bride or groom (or both) are Jews-by-choice. A Jew-by-choice is a Jew in every sphere of Jewish life, including under the *huppah*, the bridal canopy.

Your wedding also belongs to a tradition that began, according to legend, with the wedding of Adam and Eve and culminates under your *huppah*. The ritual connects you to a way of life and a system of laws as well as to each another. The celebration is yours to embellish and shape in ways that express what is unique about you as individuals and as a couple.

As you plan your wedding, it's helpful to know what parts of a Jewish wedding have religious significance and what parts are simply customary. Wearing a white wedding gown, for example, is a custom that Ashkenazic Jews borrowed from Christian neighbors during the Middle Ages; Yemenite brides to this day wear brightly colored gowns and headdresses. Thus, a Jewish bride of Indian birth can feel perfectly comfortable wearing a beautiful sari as her wedding gown. Similarly, the decorations on a *huppah* are not regulated by Jewish law; thus, one Chinese Jewish bride embroidered hers with Hebrew letters and a phoenix and a dragon, Chinese symbols for life and rebirth.[18] Your rabbi will be more than happy to answer any question that may arise as to what's "kosher" and what's not.

Brides and grooms and rabbis can even customize and personalize some parts of the wedding ceremony.[19] For instance, if the rabbi plans to address some remarks to you and your guests (and most rabbis do), you can let him or her know your preference: Would you rather avoid all mention of your conversion or do you want your guests to hear the story of your unique path to the *huppah*?

You can include your family in your Jewish wedding in ways that both honor tradition and respect people's limits. One simple and lovely way that many non-Jewish parents participate in the Jewish wedding ceremony is to walk you down the aisle. It is customary at a Jewish wedding for both sets of parents to accompany the bride and groom to the *huppah*—a gesture of bringing children into marriage rather than of giving them away. Likewise, family members and friends may be invited to hold up the *huppah* during the ceremony, or read a poem, or even sing a song.[20]

While you may suggest these options to your family, do not be disappointed if they decline. Parents who are ambivalent about a child's conversion may find it easier to take part in the nonreligious portion of the celebration instead: offering a toast at the reception, for example.

Even if your parents support your decision to convert, the prospect of attending—much more of participating in—a Jewish wedding may be daunting. Weddings are awesome enough when performed in your native language, much more so when Hebrew is involved. Prepare your non-Jewish family members with as much information as possible. Tell them what will happen at the ceremony and take your parents on a tour of the synagogue if that's where the wedding will be held. Introduce them to the rabbi, or if they live at a distance, ask your rabbi if he or she would call or write to them.

Many couples create a pamphlet that explains the Jewish symbols and prayers to their guests. This can be a wonderful tool for putting your non-Jewish family and friends at their ease. (It's also nice for Jewish guests who may know little or nothing about traditional Jewish wedding customs.) However, distributing booklets to your guests before the ceremony tends to focus attention on the page rather than on you, where it belongs. Consider handing out the booklets after the ceremony, when they can be read and discussed at leisure.

Jews-by-choice often honor their own family's ethnic traditions in the food served at the *s'eudat mitzvah*—the commanded meal that follows a wedding. Any cuisine can be prepared in a fashion that conforms to the Jewish dietary laws (*kashrut*), and a reception that features delicacies from Italy, or Japan, or Ireland, or the American South will always be remembered by your guests. (If the menu might seem at all "exotic" to Jewish family members, be sure to prepare them in advance and reassure those who need reassurance about your plans for observing the dietary laws.)

THE KETUBAH: A *ketubah* is a Jewish marriage contract that spells out the obligations of the bride and groom. It is one of the least romantic documents imaginable, and yet it has inspired centuries of artists and scribes to produce beautiful works of art. There is a large selection of illuminated and calligraphed *ketubot* (the plural) at most Judaica shops.

Some couples create or commission original *ketubot,* and decorative elements can provide another opportunity to honor your blended heritage. One artist created a Hebrew border using a passage from the Book of Ruth, "Your people shall be my people," in a subtle acknowledgment of the groom's conversion to Judaism.[21] Another included line drawings of Jerusalem and of Paris, the bride's home.

In choosing any *ketubah,* brides and grooms should consider the text as well as design and decoration. The traditional wording for a Jewish marriage contract dates from the first century C.E. and includes ancient formulas that spell out the groom's obligation to the bride. According to strictly traditional standards, if the bride is a convert to Judaism, the *ke-tubah* will refer to her as a convert, while a born-Jewish bride is described as a maiden. (There are also special designations for a previously married woman, a divorcée, and a widow.) No distinction is made in the case of a male convert, who is referred to only as the groom.[22]

Many liberal Jews use an alternative *ketubah* text, which tends to be egalitarian and spells out the mutual obligations of bride and groom. No differentiation is made when one of the partners is a convert.

Most *ketubot* have places for the names of the couple's parents, which will be entered by your rabbi on the day of the wedding. If there is a spot for English names, your own parents' names are written: James, son of Julia and Ray. However, in the space where your parents' Hebrew names appear, it is customary to enter the names of your spiritual ancestors Abraham and Sarah: Yacov ben Avraham Avienu v'Sarah Imenu. (See "Choosing a Hebrew Name.")

WHEN THE BRIDE AND GROOM ARE ALREADY HUS-BAND AND WIFE: About one third of non-Jewish spouses in interfaith marriages eventually choose to become Jewish.[23] Often, the decision to convert takes place around the time of a major life-cycle event: before the birth of a child, prior to a bar or bat mitzvah, or even following the death of a parent.[24]

Among liberal Jews, there is no requirement to have a Jewish wedding after conversion, but many couples choose to reaffirm their marriage vows under a *huppah*. These weddings tend to be intimate gatherings, and some are impromptu moments in front of the Torah with only the *bet din* present. However, some couples celebrate with small gatherings in the rabbi's office, in a synagogue sanctuary, or at the family home. These events provide a unique opportunity for children to be present at their parents' wedding and to be part of the family's rededication to Judaism.

It's entirely up to you how simple or elaborate to make this moment. You can invite guests to enjoy a meal or simply offer your witnesses a glass of champagne. Some couples buy or commission a *ketubah* for themselves and sign it before a group of witnesses. Some people exchange new wedding rings or have their old rings engraved with Hebrew words. But the entire menu of Jewish wedding rituals and customs is yours to explore and enjoy, and the overwhelming weight of Jewish tradition is on the side of more celebration, more *simcha*.

PART V

Becoming Jewish

WHAT HAPPENS AFTER THE RITUALS ARE OVER?

WILL I EVER FEEL LIKE I'M REALLY A JEW?

HOW DO I CONNECT MY ETHNIC HERITAGE WITH
MY JEWISHNESS?

DID PEOPLE CONVERT TO JUDAISM BEFORE THE
MODERN ERA?

HOW DO I FIND A SPIRITUAL HOME IN THE
JEWISH COMMUNITY?

CAN I STUDY TORAH IF I CAN'T READ HEBREW?

SHOULD I INTRODUCE MYSELF AS A JEW OR AS A
JEW-BY-CHOICE?

*B*ECOMING A JEW—CONVERTING—IS THE EASY part. Becoming Jewish—creating a Jewish identity—is a bigger challenge. Converts often report feeling lost after the formal rituals are over. There's a sense of "Now what?" or even "What have I done?" Those are normal feelings that follow most major life changes, as any new bride, groom, or parent can attest.

Creating an authentic Jewish identity for yourself takes time and patience, and, most of all, is achieved through living a Jewish life. You live a Jewish life in a hundred different ways: by doing *mitzvot*, by celebrating Jewish holidays, by joining a Jewish community, through study and, primarily, by making Jewish choices.

Creating a
Jewish Identity—
Living a
Jewish Life

ORN-JEWS RARELY UNDERSTAND THE FRAG-
ility and loneliness of the newly converted Jew. Even with all
the support in the world—from a loving partner, a helpful
rabbi, a warm congregation—it will take years before you feel
Jewish, heart and soul. Typically, Jews-by-choice are hyper-
aware of everything they don't yet know about Judaism. Some
facetiously describe the sense of having a neon sign over their
heads, flashing the word "Fake."

Jewish tradition compares converts to newborns.[1] The
metaphor is not meant to repudiate proselytes' families of origin or their past in any way, yet there is something about the
image of the newborn that speaks to the experience and vul-
nerability of a new Jew-by-choice.

Even if you've been living a Jewish life for years, conversion rituals reenact a physical birth: floating in a *mikvah* has an undeniably amniotic quality about it; ritual circumcision recalls an event that is usually performed on an eight-day-old baby; and like infants, newcomers to Judaism acquire a name. With a new name, a new status, and an exquisite understanding of how little you know about Judaism and Jewishness, you are in a tender state. Yet, you are also expected to act as guide, teacher, and exemplar to everyone around you, including your family of origin, your new Jewish family, members of your congregation, and even co-workers who suddenly turn to you to settle questions about the Jewish calendar and what Jews believe.

This is a time of transition, but unlike other life-cycle events, conversion is relatively invisible. Religion is not a subject many people are comfortable discussing, and Judaism's traditional circumspection toward converts works against you. Few people have any idea of what you're going through. Finding support is crucial, which is why joining a synagogue is so important.

But first let go of impossible expectations of yourself. Try thinking of yourself as a newly naturalized citizen in a foreign land. If you had just moved to India—even if you had prepared for the move for a long time and studied the language and culture—you probably wouldn't berate yourself for getting lost on the streets of New Delhi or for misunderstanding the niceties of the local etiquette. You certainly wouldn't be mortified because you mispronounced a word now and then. After all, it takes time to absorb a whole new culture.

In a way, you are like a new immigrant in a foreign land. You are a first-generation Jew, staking your claim to a future in new territory. As many first-generation immigrants to the United States can tell you, your appreciation of the benefits and responsibilities of "citizenship" will likely be keener than that of born-Jews. And that may even include your own children, who will take their Judaism for granted in ways you never can.

However, the image of nationality doesn't convey the magnitude of this change. Converts are also like transplanted flowers, setting down roots in new soil. It may be years before you are acclimated to the elements, before you take hold, thrive, and blossom. Some converts blend right in, indistinguishable from the natives even before their roots are established. Others add colors and textures that enrich the Jewish garden in unexpected ways.

Whatever metaphor suits you best—neonate, newcomer, green sprout—remember that beginnings are rarely easy. Eventually, you will feel at home. Time is your ally.

Time alone, however, cannot resolve all issues of ethnicity. American Jews still tend to behave as though there were only one authentic cultural expression of Judaism, which tastes, smells, and sounds like the Judaism of nineteenth-century Eastern Europe. But if your name is O'Hara, or if you are of Asian or African ancestry, there is no way to "pass" as an Eastern European–type Jew. And why would you want to? The unique combination of your birthright and your Judaism is a point of pride to be handed down to your children. And like others before you, you can create an authentic Jewish identity while affirming your ethnic heritage.

Converts knit their dual identities together in all sorts of ways. Studying the history and traditions of the Jewish community in the land of your national origin is one way to connect the two. Another is to weave the crafts, colors, and flavors of your native traditions into the unfolding tapestry of Jewish life in your holiday and life-cycle observances. For example:

- On the occasion of her conversion, a young woman from India made a wall hanging that included both Jewish symbols and *shisha* mirrors, a traditional element in Indian embroidery.

- An African-American Jewish family always seeks out fruits imported from Africa for their Tu B'shvat seder.

- A Danish Jewish father decorates his family's *sukkah* with the Scandinavian straw figures he inherited from his grandmothers.

Ethnic chauvinism is declining in the Jewish community, partly due to the presence of so many Jews-by-choice and partly because of a growing appreciation of the long history of Jewish pluralism. While the Broadway and Hollywood Yiddishkeit of novelist Sholem Aleichem's *Fiddler on the Roof* [2] continues to be a sentimental touchstone, there is widespread curiosity about the varieties of Jewish experience. The Ladino music of Spain, for instance, has joined Eastern European klezmer as part of regular Jewish concert fare. Menus from

Persia, Italy, and Egypt—redolent of lemon and garlic—are featured in newspaper articles about how to cook a Passover seder. Mediterranean Jews and the Jewish communities of northern Africa are the subject of new books every year, and visitors to Israel are always struck by the diversity of Jewish culture in a nation where Yemenite and Ethiopian communities cherish cuisines, musical traditions, and religious customs that bear no resemblance to the world of the *shtetl*.

Nevertheless, being a hyphenated Jew in America is not always easy. A born-Jew who hangs up lights in the shapes of dreidels and six-pointed stars during Hanukkah may do so with impunity. But a Jew-by-choice who does the same thing may worry about seeming to create a Jewish version of Christmas. It's not easy to gain enough Jewish self-confidence to overcome a need to justify your Jewish choices. And sadly, it's not just a matter of paranoia. In the words of Rabbi Adin Steinsaltz, "The hardest thing about becoming a Jew is the Jews."[3]

At the beginning of her book, *Your People, My People: Finding Acceptance and Fulfillment as a Jew by Choice,* Lena Romanoff tells a story about buying food for a homebound non-Jewish neighbor. When a Jewish acquaintance saw the neighbor's pork roast in Romanoff's shopping cart, she berated her—and all converts—as "false" Jews. Romanoff had been Jewish long enough to shrug off the insult, but for someone just establishing a Jewish identity, that kind of encounter can be devastating, even if you know that Jewish law expressly forbids Jews from saying such horrible things. If such a thing happens to you, don't let it fester; talk to your rabbi, your Jewish friends, and members of your temple. Injustice and prejudice thrive on silence.

Closer to home, getting used to Jews' ethnic style can present a challenge, too. Although there are plenty of cool, distant Jewish families, Jewish households tend to be demonstrative, overinvolved, and "hot." One woman, reared in a Protestant home with roots dating back to the *Mayflower*, recalls being stunned at the difference between the etiquette of her parents' home and the manners displayed at her in-laws' table: the getting up and sitting down during meals, the volume and passion of the conversation, the painstaking discussion about every dish served, the freedom to comment upon other people's appearance and demeanor. "I knew I wasn't in Kansas anymore," she says. (Woody Allen covered the flip side of this image with the midwestern Thanksgiving dinner scene in *Annie Hall*.)

The woman who was so discomfited by her in-laws' table is now able to enjoy and participate in that hurly-burly. Nevertheless, she doubts that she will overcome the upbringing that taught her to maintain a stiff upper lip during illness. "My husband has no trouble complaining and asking for anything when he's got the flu. I can't imagine doing that."

While many issues raised by ethnic differences are minor, some mutually instructive, and some just plain funny, they occasionally do lead to real marital problems—especially if your communication styles are out of sync. In such cases, you might seek out a spiritually sensitive therapist or a counselor who is familiar with the field of ethnotherapy, which takes into account the importance of cultural differences.[4]

Your Mitzvot

IF JUDAISM SEEMS RELATIVELY UNINTERESTED in matters of faith, it is passionately concerned with the details of life and righteous behavior. "The act of giving food to a helpless child is meaningful regardless of whether or not the moral intention is present," wrote Abraham Joshua Heschel. "God asks for the heart, and we must spell out our answer in terms of deeds."[5]

The deeds God requires are called *mitzvot,* Hebrew for "commandments" or "good deeds." But *mitzvah* is more complicated than either translation suggests. A *mitzvah* is what Jews do in response to the divine. A *mitzvah* is value-in-action—a deed filled with good. *Mitzvot* are the praxis of Judaism.

According to tradition, Jews are obligated to perform the 613 *mitzvot* found in the Torah. Liberal Jews tend to approach every *mitzvah* with a combination of respect and curiosity as each one presents an occasion for reflection and for choice. Rabbi Arnold Jacob Wolf uses an interesting image to describe the process of embracing *mitzvot*. He described them as "jewels" embedded in the Jewish path; as you walk along, you reach down to pick up these gems and discover that some come up rather easily. "Don't murder" isn't much of a problem for most people. "Don't eat shellfish" and "Honor your mother and father" are a bit more challenging.

At any given time, a *mitzvah* may seem too deeply embedded for you to pry it out of the ground. And yet, there comes a day when you discover that a *mitzvah* that seemed immovable just months earlier is now loose: *kashrut*, for example, no longer seems an arbitrary and arcane system of prohibitions but is a meaningful reminder that everything—including eating—can be opportunity to find and create holiness.

As a Jew, you are obliged to grapple with the *mitzvot* and to discover which ones evoke in you a sense of being commanded—a feeling of "I don't think I can skip this one anymore." As a liberal Jew, you are free to experiment with the *mitzvot* and to discover how to make them your own. But you are also obliged to act upon what you learn.

Take, for example, the *mitzvah* of making Shabbat, which is one of the loveliest, most accessible, and rewarding aspects of Jewish life. Shabbat is an island of peace, a weekly vacation, an affirmation of everything that is good in your life. The Hebrew essayist and Zionist leader Ahad Ha'am wrote,

"More than the Jews have kept Shabbat, Shabbat has kept the Jews."

If the "jewel" of Shabbat is not yet part of your life, it's a good one to reach for. Begin by lighting candles on Friday night, then try to avoid running errands on Saturday morning, and make time for the ones you love on Saturday afternoon. Your Shabbat observance may begin by reading about the meaning and practice of the Sabbath, which is, in itself, a *mitzvah*.

Indeed, study—especially Torah study—is traditionally considered the most important *mitzvah*.[6] For Jews, prayer, community, and study are inseparable, as intertwined as the braids of dough on a loaf of challah. In many ways, study with others is the quintessential expression of Jewish spirituality. (See the chapters "Study" and "Your Torah.")

Of course, not every Jew is a reader, and there are *mitzvot* and learning opportunities to suit the interests and abilities of everyone. The *mitzvot* concerned with helping the needy, healing the sick, freeing the captive, and making peace are incumbent on all Jews. You can fulfill the *mitzvah* of feeding the hungry by working in a synagogue-supported soup kitchen or by setting up a canned-food drive in your own congregation. The *mitzvah* of building up the Jewish community can be performed in hundreds of ways, from fund-raising for the local federation to volunteering for a committee in your synagogue. The precept of *hiddur mitzvah*, of beautifying the commandments, opens the way for artists to embellish Jewish life according to their talents. Holiday observance is a *mitz-*

vah, too, and every year brings new opportunities for learning and for creating your own Jewish traditions.

It is not the responsibility of any Jew to finish or master any of the *mitzvot.* On the other hand, none of us are free to stop trying.[7]

Your Torah

ℬECOMING A JEW MEANS TAKING POSSESSION of the Torah and finding meaning in it. Torah is a mainstay of Jewish life and one of its great pleasures. According to tradition, the Jewish people came into being when God gave them the Torah, and its study has defined and sustained them ever since. For Jews, prayer and Torah study are on the same spiritual plane because both are seen as ways to encounter the holy. In his conversion memoir, Julius Lester writes, "For me, studying Torah is an act of engaging God with my imagination, my reason, and my feeling."[8]

"The Torah" refers to the first five books of the Hebrew Bible, and "Torah" can refer to the entire Hebrew Bible, to all Jewish commentary on the Bible, to the entire library of Jewish thought, and even to the idea of revelation itself.[9] "Torah study," however, refers specifically to the close reading of the first five books of the Bible: Genesis, Exodus, Leviticus, Numbers, and Deuteronomy.

Torah study is a wonderful introduction to the Jewish approach to scripture and to the passionate give-and-take of Jewish pedagogy. It is also a doorway to the community and a way to find your place in the Jewish world.

Most synagogues run weekly Torah study sessions—informal, drop-in conversations usually held on Saturday morning prior to Shabbat services. Over coffee and bagels, people gather to discuss the weekly Torah portion, often under the guidance of a rabbi or other teacher. Sometimes the group leader will bring in a rabbinic commentary to focus the discussion, but often the conversation flows from the interests and questions of the people gathered on that given day.[10] Torah study groups are great fun. In the course of an hour, the conversation may range from Maimonides to Mel Brooks, from sibling rivalry to local politics, from temple politics to the existence of God. If your week seems crowded with small talk, Torah study releases you into big talk.

Don't be afraid to attend a Torah study group because you don't know enough or won't be able to keep up with everyone else. Most of the other people at the table don't read Hebrew either, and many of them won't have read the Torah portion in advance. Besides, Jewish tradition holds that any reader might discover or reveal some new insight into the text unimagined by anyone else in history. Just as the Torah was given in the wilderness—not within the boundaries of any nation or even within the land God promised to the Hebrews—the Torah is open and available to anyone.

If you grew up reading the Bible as a Christian, Torah study can be a bit of a shock, not just theologically but in the way Jews tend to manhandle the text. Torah study is not deferential or worshipful: humor and anger are not only permitted, they are encouraged. So are arguing, wrestling, imagining, and interjecting contemporary dilemmas into ancient settings. All of these are part of the process called *midrash*, which means "search."

Week after week, generation after generation, century after century, Jews have infused the Torah with new life through *midrash*, which begins with two assumptions: first, that the biblical text is sacred and has something of ultimate importance to say to everyone—not just rabbis and scholars; and second, that the Torah's message is not obvious but hidden, so that people have to work at it, play in it, seek it out.

Midrash has been the *modus operandi* of Torah study for nearly two thousand years. Rabbi Abraham Joshua Heschel even suggested that the whole Torah could be understood as *midrash:* less a photographic record than a series of handmade illustrations. The story of Sinai, for instance, was written down 600 to 700 years after the Hebrews left Egypt, which means that the story we read today was filtered through the lens of a culture radically different from the one it describes. Thus, even when it was brand-new, this text was never an end in itself but an attempt at discerning contemporary meaning from an ancient story.

Midrash is one of the primary ways that Jews have gotten sustenance from the Torah, which is called "a tree of life."[11] *Midrash aggadah*—the search for stories—is how Jews have filled in the blank spaces in the biblical narrative. An entire rabbinical literature of such stories, collectively called "the Midrash," takes remarkable liberties with the text, imagining whole scenes and conversations that seem "missing" from the written record. For instance, the Torah sketches out the scene where Cain and Abel stand together in a field before Cain kills his brother, but tells nothing about their conversation. Did they quarrel? Did they fight? The rabbis invented alternative dialogues and motivations to fill the gaping hole in the story, and Jews have been debating those theories and coming up with more ideas ever since.[12]

In addition to its legal and interpretive uses, *midrash* can also be a source of personal inspiration and instruction. *Midrash* asks that you, the reader, bring all of yourself to Torah study: your childhood, your family, your doubts, strengths, and expertise. Studying the story of Cain and Abel can prompt reflection upon sibling relationships, your own or those of your children. Rabbi Norman J. Cohen writes, "Whenever a passionate reader grants any text an appropriate reading, an interpretation or expansion which helps him or her as a human being, and fosters growth, the Torah will come alive. At that instant it will be working in the life of that very reader."[13]

But talking about *midrash* is a little bit like discussing good food: it leaves you hungry for the real thing. What follows is an appetizer—a story based upon the biblical account of Abraham's break from his family, especially his father, Terah.[14]

Abraham the Convert: A Midrash

Now these are the begettings of Terah.
Terah begot Avram,* Nahor and Haran;
and Haran begot Lot.
Haran died in the living presence of Terah his father
in the land of his kindred, in Ur of the Chaldeans.[15]

Although Avram is presented as Terah's oldest, we actually learn more about his youngest son, Haran, who dies in the "living presence" of his father. Given the choice of words, it's hard not to imagine Terah cradling his youngest son's head on his deathbed, or to feel the pain of the parent who loses a child. If Avram was present at this scene, surely he felt his father's suffering, and perhaps he resolved to do everything he could to protect his sobbing dad from feeling such devastating pain again. And perhaps that is why Avram cannot leave his father's house until after Terah dies:

And the days of Terah were five years and two hundred
years,
then Terah died,

---

*Abraham begins the story as Abram—in Hebrew, Avram. It is only when he makes his covenant with God that his name is changed to Abraham. Likewise, Sarai becomes Sarah.

in Harran.
YHWH said to Avram:
Go-you-forth
from your land
from your kindred,
from your father's house
to the land that I will let you see.[16]

God tells Avram exactly what he is leaving behind: the old neighborhood, all of his cousins, the house he grew up in—a list that underscores how much he has to set aside and how difficult it will be to go.

Virtually everyone who has converted to Judaism has felt cut off from the comforts of home. Every Jew-by-choice considers the impact of his or her choice on family—especially parents. Converts often voice their fears, real and imagined, about how their choice might hurt their parents: "I know they think I would be rejecting them and abandoning the values I was raised with." Or even, "My father would die if I told him I was going to leave the church."

With Terah dead, Avram was spared having to explain his choice. He did not have to break the heart of a father who had already suffered the loss of a beloved son, the baby of the family. Avram did not lie awake at night searching for the right words, wondering how to say:

"Dad, try to see that my decision is not a repudiation of you or our family. I'm doing this because I'm following the voice of God. And in a way, I'm even fulfilling your own dreams. Didn't you once set out for Canaan, too? Well, I will finish the journey for you. I'm not rejecting you. I will be taking you with me.

"Your memory will always be a guide and a light unto my feet. Your family will always be my family. In fact, if Sarai and I are ever blessed with a son, we will send him back here to find a bride from among your people—who will always be my people, too.

"Please, Dad. Try to understand. I'm only doing what I have to do, and what is right for me. But that doesn't mean that I don't love you. I'm your son and I will always love you."

Community
Matters

$\mathcal{Y}$OU CANNOT BE JEWISH IN ISOLATION. TORAH study is a communal enterprise, not a solitary pursuit. There are no Jewish hermits or monasteries. Community is as fundamental to Judaism as monotheism, which is why so many Jewish prayers can only be recited in the presence of a *minyan*, a quorum of ten adults.

Lighting candles every Friday night, reading Jewish books, sending money to Jewish organizations, celebrating the holidays with your family, and observing the laws of *kashrut* may be deeply meaningful. But there is a limit to how much anyone can learn or grow without teachers or fellow students. There is a limit to how much you can "repair the world" or help other people without finding partners for the work. There is a limit to any individual's strength in the face of loss and sorrow. The way that Jews expand these limits on learning, growth, giving, and receiving is by joining a synagogue.

A synagogue is a *beit k'nesset*, a house of assembly, a social center; it is also a *beit midrash*, a house of study, a place to search and learn; and it is a *beit tefilah*, a house of prayer, a sanctuary.[17]

Becoming part of a congregation provides all kinds of opportunities to develop and nurture your Jewish identity. Attending services will familiarize you with Jewish worship so that you will eventually feel at home with the words and melodies, the rhythms and customs of public prayer. Belonging to a temple makes it easier to continue your Jewish education since congregations typically offer a wide range of classes, from Torah study and Hebrew language courses, to holiday and life-cycle workshops, to concerts of Jewish music and holiday cooking classes, to lectures about Jewish history, Israeli politics, and Jewish humor. The list is endless.

Synagogues create community, providing you with opportunities to meet and work with people who are very much like you and people who couldn't be more different. Many congregations encourage members to form small *havurot*— groups that meet to celebrate holidays, study, and socialize, and which often come to function as extended families.

In most cases, Jews-by-choice find their communal home in the synagogue of the rabbi who converted them. But given the mobility of American society and the fact that many people convert as young adults, you may eventually find yourself looking for a congregational home.

Finding the right synagogue for you may take some time, but it's worth the effort. Shop for a congregation by attending services, reading the membership literature, talking to members, and setting up a meeting with the rabbi. Look for a temple that suits your needs for community (are there other young couples, singles, young families?), intellectual growth (what does the adult education program look like?), and spirituality (how do services make you feel?). Is the congregation intimate and informal? Is the synagogue large enough to offer the kind of programs and services you need?

As a Jew-by-choice shopping for a congregation, you might ask whether the congregation has an Outreach (Reform) or Keruv (Conservative) committee, which run programs for interfaith families, prospective Jews-by-choice, and converts. Ask whether the committee is active. What kind of programs does it offer? Are mentors available for new Jews? Is the rabbi supportive of the committee's work? The presence of a healthy Outreach or Keruv committee points to congregational diversity and a welcoming stance. However, the presence or absence of such a committee should not be a litmus test. Since congregational activities tend to depend upon volunteer time and energy, most committees wax and wane over the years. If the rabbi or membership chair welcomes your questions about Outreach or Keruv and asks whether you would like to work on such a committee, you may have the opportunity to make an important contribution to the community even as you help yourself.

Congregations do not, as a rule, encourage Jews-by-choice to establish permanent groups or *havurot* for fear of institutionalizing any separation between born-Jews and converts. The goal of every rabbi and synagogue is to have Jews-by-choice become fully integrated into the community.

Your First Year as a Jew

CONVERTING TO JUDAISM IS A LITTLE BIT LIKE getting married. Like a wedding, a conversion marks a profound change in your personal status. It marks the end of one period in your life and the beginning of another. Even if you've been living a Jewish life for years, even if becoming a Jew feels more like a homecoming than a transformation, this rite of passage—like all life-cycle events—carries a share of confusion, conflict, and unanticipated consequences. Stress is in the nature of change.

According to Jewish custom, brides and grooms remain brides and grooms for a full year. Only after your first wedding anniversary—after a full year's seasons and a full cycle of Jewish holidays—do you become husband and wife.

Jews-by-choice may also experience a liminal period, a time of change and adjustment, that follows the formal commitment. While most converts report that it takes substantially more than twelve months before you feel comfortable calling yourself a Jew, the first year is nevertheless filled with milestones.

Some rabbis refer new Jews to mentors—often another convert who understands what you're feeling. A mentor can be someone who walks you through a year's worth of holidays, attends services with you, and/or invites you to his or her home for Shabbat. A good match (in Yiddish, *shidduch*) between you and your mentor can make the difference between comfort and confusion. If mentoring for new Jews is not yet part of your congregation's regular repertoire of services, bring up the possibility with the rabbi and appropriate committee chair.

Outreach or Keruv committees in some congregations provide forums for Jews-by-choice and those considering conversion. Sometimes, a support group is the only place to get satisfying answers to questions that may arise: Will I ever really feel Jewish? What's the best way to involve non-Jewish grandparents in the preparations for my son's bar mitzvah? How does it feel to sit *shiva* for a Christian parent? Am I supposed to stop liking gospel music once I become a Jew?

The Jewish Converts Network, a private, nonprofit, nondenominational organization, runs support groups for new and prospective converts. The group is based in the Philadelphia area, but its founder and director, Lena Romanoff, has trained support-group facilitators around the country and can put you in touch with local resources. "No one should go through conversion alone," says Romanoff.*

Whether or not you choose to join or start a support group, you might want to keep a journal of your first year as a Jew. Time your entries according to the Jewish calendar: just before Shabbat every week, or at the start of every Hebrew month, or during every holiday. Take photographs at holiday celebrations and begin a pictorial history of your Jewish life. Stay in touch with your rabbi, and if you aren't a member of his or her congregation, call or write a letter from time to time.

Your first Christmas as a Jew may seem especially difficult. Most Jews-by-choice visit their non-Jewish families at Christmas, where they exchange gifts and participate in the nonreligious traditions of the seasons. However, if it seems too painful to spend your first Christmas at a sibling's house that's sure to be filled with tinsel, arrange to spend Thanksgiving or New Year's together instead. You may be better able to enjoy Christmas there another year. Like many other aspects of your Jewish life, your reactions to Christmas will change over time.

Regardless of whether you spend any part of December with your family of origin, you still face lots of choices: Do you use generic holiday cards and wrapping paper and ask family members to do the same? What kind of holiday card should you send to your seventy-five-year-old Catholic grandmother? Is it okay to send Christmas cards to Christian relatives? You'll probably get your best advice and suggestions from seasoned Jews-by-choice.

See listing in Resources.

One common concern is how children might react to a Christmas visit to Grandma's house. However, one of the lessons of early childhood is that "my family does things its own way." If parents are clear and nondefensive, most kids understand that celebrating Christmas at Grandma and Grandpa's house is like going to a friend's house for a birthday party: you enjoy the cake and ice cream, give a gift, and accept a party favor. But when you go back to your house, the celebration is over because it isn't *your* birthday. It's an explanation that a six-year-old child can understand, but it's also a rationale that may help satisfy the six-year-old inside of you, who remembers when Christmas was your party, too.

When you reach the anniversary of your conversion, make the day special. Prepare or go out for a special meal, ask for an *aliyah* at your temple, go and buy yourself the Jewish book you've been meaning to read, go for a walk and think about how your life's journey brought you to this moment, or write a letter to your rabbi and describe your first year as a Jew.

Take a long, deep breath and recite the *shehehiyanu*:

Baruch ata Adonai Eloheynu melech ha-olam, shehehiyanu vekiamanu, vehigianu lazman hazeh.

Holy One of Blessing, Your Presence Fills Creation, You have kept us alive, You have sustained us, You have brought us to this moment.

Who Needs to Know?

Some Jews-by-choice take great pride in their decision to convert and get a kick out of seeing how other people react when they explain how Macmillan came to be a Jewish name. Others resent any reference to their conversion and squirm when the rabbi points out that the president of the congregation was born a Lutheran.

Some synagogues treat conversion like all other life-cycle events, publishing announcements of conversions in newsletters and on bulletin boards. Other temples treat conversions far more discreetly, and officially nobody but the rabbi, family, and close friends know who is converting, or who is a Jew-by-choice.

In practice, it's fairly common for both approaches to co-exist within the same congregation. Rabbis usually do their best to maintain the privacy of converts who wish their decision to stay within the immediate family—even if full disclosure is the custom in the congregation. Likewise, if you want an *aliyah* in honor of your conversion, most rabbis will arrange it gladly, even if it's never been done before in that particular congregation.

Ultimately, you must do what is comfortable for you. However, if you don't mind talking about your decision to become a Jew, you are in a unique position to change Jewish attitudes and practices. Jews-by-choice who "go public" teach and inspire and turn the abstract principle of Judaism's openness to converts into a flesh-and-blood reality. You remind other Jews that there is more than one way to make new Jews. And you show non-Jews in your congregation that the door is open to them, too.

Most important, you challenge the way all Jews think about themselves and the future of Judaism. Converts embody a new paradigm of Jewishness for the twenty-first century. While it's become a cliché to say "We are all Jews by choice," the meaning of that phrase comes to life in you, your family, and your children. You demonstrate that ethnicity, nostalgia, and guilt are not what keeps Judaism alive; that choice and commitment are the real source of Jewish vitality.

A great many people are already teaching these lessons. As more people choose Judaism and as more congregations and families are enriched by the enthusiasm and knowledge of Jews-by-choice, conversion is beginning to be viewed as just another interesting bit of information—like the fact that some members of the temple were born in South Africa, or that someone spent time in a Buddhist ashram. A non-Jewish background will probably always be a fascinating and salient fact when Jews get acquainted and swap family stories. But conversion has long since stopped being a conversation-stopper.

You are a Jew. And like other Jews, your talents and questions and your children will change the course of Jewish history. But as a Jew-by-choice you also bring something unprecedented and wonderful into the world: you cause a new *mitzvah* to come into being. Because of you, all Jews are now obliged and privileged to provide *hachnasat ha-ger*—hospitality for converts, or literally, "the bringing in of the convert." Because of you, there is a new opportunity to bring holiness into the world by showing *kavod ha-ger*, respect for the convert.

Baruch ha-ba. Blessed is your coming, brother.
Bruchah ha-ba'ah. Blessed is your coming, sister.

PART VI

Your History

A Short History

of Conversion

to Judaism

Biblical Times:
2500 B.C.E. – 300 B.C.E.

IN THE BEGINNING, there was no such thing as "Judaism" and the word "conversion" would have been an anachronism. And yet, the early Hebrew tribes and later the Israelites who settled in Canaan did attract and welcome new members. The Bible contains many stories about people who joined the tribe, nearly always through marriage, as was the case with Sarah, the first Jewish woman.

Although the Torah describes Abraham as having a direct relationship with God, Sarah's connection to God and the covenant is mediated through her husband. At least at the beginning of their journey, she goes because he goes. One contemporary poet imagines Sarah's "conversion" through the eyes of a present-day Jew-by choice:

> I began this journey because I loved one Jew.
> I sometimes imagine that, at least at first,
> our ancestor Sarah might have done the same,
> following her man from Haran to Canaan
> through all the hardships and terrors of ancient travel
> because she loved him no matter what his ideas or voices
> or perhaps precisely *because of* his ideas and voices.[1]

Among the many others who married into the Jewish people and transformed its history is Asenath, the Egyptian wife of Joseph and mother of Ephraim and Menashe, whose names are mentioned in the traditional Friday night blessing for sons.[2] Tamar, daughter-in-law and then wife to Judah, gave birth to Perez, an ancestor of King David. Indeed, the Bible contains a remarkable number of important non-Jewish wives (Zipporah, a Midianite, was married to Moses) and non-Jewish mothers of heroic Jewish sons: Sarah, Asenath, Tamar, Ruth. Rechab, a prostitute who aided Joshua, is named as the mother of Jonadab and honored by the tradition.[3]

Israelite society seemed willing to grant full membership to anyone who wanted it, regardless of his or her past. Slaves and the children of slaves became equals, as did foreigners of all descriptions. Indeed, Ruth, the most famous convert, is an example of how conversion was an option for anyone—even the hereditary enemies of the tribe. Ruth was not only a gentile, she was a Moabite, a tribe that the Torah forbade as marriage partners to the Jews.[4] The rabbis made much of the fact that Ruth the Moabite was an ancestor of King David, from whose line the messiah is to come.

Although the most commonly trod path, marriage was not the only way that non-Hebrews became members of the tribe in biblical times. The people who accompanied Abraham and Sarah from Haran, the first generation of Jews, could be called converts—people who left their parents' homes and religious traditions for a radically different life. Several generations later, when Moses brought the Torah down from Sinai, its laws were accepted not only by the Israelite descendants of Abraham and Sara but also by non-Jews who left Egypt with the Hebrews—called the "mixed multitude"[5] in the Torah.

In other words, converts were present at Sinai—the crucial encounter that transformed a tribe of Hebrews into the Jewish people.

The rituals and laws of conversion were not formalized during biblical times. Hundreds of years later, the rabbis who wrote the Talmud embroidered tales of ritual immersion and circumcision around the multitudes at Sinai. But conversion in those days was a process of assimilation and naturalization, of accepting the norms and rules of Hebrew culture and giving up other beliefs and practices. At some point in history, those who wished to change their status from *ger*[6] (stranger) to *Yisrael* may have been asked to make a sacrifice to the God of Israel. Or perhaps all it took to become a member of the tribe was a declaration of intent. Indeed, Ruth's famous speech to Naomi, "Whither thou goest, I will go," may have been a formal statement of conversion. Whatever was required of adults, however, their children automatically became full members of the community.

In the later writings, the Bible gives voice to the tension between the desire to welcome strangers and the need to maintain a discrete Jewish identity. The prophets Ezra and Nehemiah railed against intermarriage, for example. Their complaint was not against all foreign-born wives, however, but against those who did not adopt the customs of the Israelites and maintained their pagan practices; in essence, the prophets were insisting on the need for sincere conversion.[7]

Rabbinic / Talmudic Period: 300 B.C.E. – 500 C.E.

THIS RELATIVELY SHORT span of Jewish history was the first golden age of conversion to Judaism—which by that time understood and called them conversions. According to some scholars, the Jewish population, which was no more than 150,000 in 586 B.C.E., grew to eight million by the first century of the Common Era—a huge increase that was due in some measure to the large number of proselytes.[8] Understandably, this was also a period when Jewish thought and law about conversion was debated and codified.

During the Second Commonwealth (538 B.C.E.–70 C.E.), Jews rebuilt the Temple and resumed its practices, and Jewish influence was probably at its peak in the ancient world. Some of the Jewish soldiers who had served in Alexander's army stayed in Alexandria, married Egyptian women, and established a large community there. Philo, an Alexandrine Jewish philosopher of the first century C.E., estimates that there were a million Jews in Egypt—about one eighth of the population.[9] Other communities were established in Syria and Rome, where a number of synagogues were established by freed Jewish slaves. At one point, 10 percent of the Roman Empire, roughly four million people, may have been converts to Judaism.

Although there were no missionaries or any organized effort at proselytizing, many gentiles were impressed with the example set by Jews in the Diaspora. Flavius Josephus, a Jewish historian of the day, wrote, "There is not a city of the Grecians, nor any of the barbarians, nor any nation whatsoever, whither our custom of resting on the seventh day has not come, and by which our fasts and lighting up lamps and many of our prohibitions as to food are not observed."

This period left a record of names and stories about converts: King Boas of Arabia converted in order to marry Salome, the sister of King Herod; the conversion of the entire royal family of Adiabene was said to have been instigated by Queen Helene, who was taught by a Jewish merchant named Hanania; Fulvia, the wife of Saturnius, a Roman senator, was also moved by a lay teacher to become a Jew; Flavius Clemens, a nephew of the Roman emperor Vespasian and himself a Roman consul, also accepted the God of Israel.

The religious beliefs of the Jews were disseminated through books as well as by example. Philo wrote *De Vita Mosis,* about the life of Moses as an introduction to the ideals of Judaism for interested outsiders. Two converts translated the Torah into the global languages of the era: Onkelos into Aramaic, Aquila into Greek.

The only cases of forced conversion also date from this era. John Hyrcanus, a Hasmonean ruler, defeated the Edomites in 125 B.C.E. and demanded that they become Jews; his son Aristobulus I did the same to the Itureans in 105 B.C.E. But these incidents were exceptional, condemned by the rabbis and never repeated. Converts came of their own free will, drawn by the exemplary behavior of Jews, attracted by Jewish teachings, and in response to the welcome the seekers found in the community. In fact, so many people were attracted to the faith of the Jews that in 139 B.C.E. the praetor of Rome banished them from his city, "because they tried to corrupt Roman morals through their cult." Later, during the first century, the Flavians, apparently alarmed by the success of the Jews, made circumcision a capital offense.

This influx of converts posed a challenge to the Jewish community—a challenge that was met in very different ways by the two competing schools of Jewish thought, embodied by the famous dueling rabbis, Shammai and Hillel:

> *A gentile came before Shammai and said to him, "Take me as a proselyte, but only if you teach me the entire Torah, all of it, while I stand on one foot." Shammai threw him out, hitting him with a builder's measuring rod that he happened to have in his hand.*
>
> *When the same person came to Hillel with the same demand, Hillel said to him, "What is hateful to you, do not do to you fellow man. This is the entire Torah, all of it. The rest is commentary. Go and study it."*

Likewise:

> *A certain gentile once came before Shammai and asked him, "How many Torahs do you have?"*
>
> *"Two," replied Shammai. "The Written Torah and the Oral Torah."[10]*
>
> *The man said, "I will believe you about the Written Torah, but not about the Oral Torah. Take me as a proselyte, but only teach me the Written Torah." Shammai scolded him and angrily ordered him to get out.*
>
> *When this person went to Hillel with the same de-*

mand, Hillel accepted him as a proselyte. On the first day, the master taught his student the letters of the alphabet in order: alef, bet, gimmel, dalet—all the way to tav. But the following day, he reversed the order of the letters.

"But yesterday you did not teach them to me in this order," the gentile protested.

Hillel replied, "If you will depend upon me for the order of the letters, you must also rely upon me for the validity of the Oral Torah."[11]

Hillel's good-natured and patient acceptance of the seeker typified Jewish reaction to the convert at the beginning of the Common Era.[12] The Talmud does contain some negative and even nasty comments about proselytes, but these may have been no more than a response to the practice of Roman spies, who pretended to convert in order to uncover Jewish plans for rebellion. The vast majority of comments about converts in the Talmud and the Midrash are favorable, and some are downright rhapsodic:

The convert is dearer to God than Israel. When the nation assembled at the foot of Mount Sinai, Israel would not have accepted the Torah without seeing the thunders and the lightning and the quaking mountain and hearing the sound of the shofar. Whereas the proselyte, without a single miracle, consecrated himself to the Holy One, praised be He, and puts upon himself the yoke of the kingdom of heaven. Can anyone be deemed more worthy of God's love?[13]

And perhaps the most remarkable statement about the importance of converts: "God dealt kindly with Israel in scattering them among the nations for, because of this, proselytes were added to Israel."[14]

The Talmud also set out the ritual requirements for conversion that have remained in effect ever since. Although there were dissenting opinions, the majority ruled that men had to be circumcised, and both males and females were required to undergo ritual immersion and give a Temple offering (in the days when the Temple still stood). The rabbis thought that converts should first be discouraged by pointing out the added obligations of Jewish life and the fact that conversion was not a precondition for salvation, since any righteous person, regardless of his or her religion, had a place in the world to come.[15]

Nevertheless, if a seeker persisted, the rabbis said that the basics of the tradition were to be explained in simple language; after that, the primary consideration in accepting a convert was sincerity. Although there were some limits placed on converts' participation—they could not, for instance, marry priests or hold public office—the rabbis insisted upon the full equality of converts in an era when hereditary status was still a lingering fact of life. "Whoever is part of the congregation, including even proselytes who devote themselves to Torah, they are just as important as the High Priest."[16]

In 70 C.E., the Second Temple was destroyed by the Romans and the Jews lost their national home. The Jews who were sent into exile in Babylonia, however, were permitted to practice their national religion, and the Babylonian exile fundamentally transformed Judaism from a tribal, Temple-centered, and priest-led rite into a universal faith based on prayer and study, unmediated by priests. God became portable and the Torah became available to anyone who accepted its laws—and apparently many did. Isaiah called the non-Israelites who accepted the teachings of the Jews in Babylon "those who joined themselves to the Lord."[17]

Jewish warmth toward proselytes cooled in direct proportion to changes in the political climate of the times. In 306 C.E., Christianity became the state religion of the Roman Empire, and although Judaism itself was not outlawed, within a few hundred years it became illegal for Jews to accept converts. Thus, the first golden age of conversion to Judaism came to an end.

The Middle Ages:
500 C.E. – 1800 C.E.

FOR MOST OF this long period, Jews were a pariah people. Edicts from Rome to Mecca to London barred Jews from doing certain kinds of work, sometimes forced them to wear strange clothes, and forbade them from proselytizing—often under penalty of death. Although Jews never sent out missionaries, the unending stream of proselytes and the steady promulgation of laws against "Judaizing" testify to the fact that even when it was dangerous, conversion never ceased. One historian estimates that approximately fifteen thousand people converted to Judaism in Europe between 1000 and 1200.[18]

This was a very dangerous thing to do. The Christian

church considered it apostasy, a form of heresy that was not merely an error but a capital crime. According to one medieval law code, *Las siete partidas* (1260) of Alfonso X of Castile, "Where a Christian is so unfortunate as to become a Jew, we order that he shall be put to death."[19]

Nevertheless, Judaism continued to attract a procession of clergymen who ascribed their conversions to comparative readings of the Hebrew and Christian Bibles. Among these was Bishop Alemann Bodo, court chaplain to the Frankish emperor Louis I. In 839, Bodo fled to Muslim Spain, where conversion from Christianity to Judaism was not illegal. Another priest-convert from southern Italy, Obadiah, claimed that he was inspired by the story of yet another proselyte, Andreas, the archbishop of Bari. Obadiah died in Egypt in 1078.[20]

Some converts were martyred on account of their choice. From 1264 there is a record of "Abraham, son of Abraham our Father, of Ishpurk, who rejected the gods of the nations, broke the heads of the idols, and was tormented with severe tortures." In 1270, another Abraham, son of Abraham, a former monk, was burned in Weissenburg. In 1539, Malcher, the converted wife of a Kraków alderman, was put to the stake. And as late as July 15, 1738, two Russians were burned in a public square in St. Petersburg: a born-Jew, Baruch Liebov, and the convert he was accused of having influenced—Alexander Voznitzin, a retired naval captain.[21]

As Baruch Liebov's death demonstrates, the convert was not the only one at risk. Jews and even entire Jewish communities could be punished when a conversion was discovered or even suspected. After Wecelinus, a German priest, converted to Judaism and went to live with the Jews of Mainz in about 1005, all the Jews of the city were expelled. From the eleventh century comes the story of a French woman from a wealthy family who made her way to Narbonne, where she converted and married Rabbi David. But her family pursued her, and eventually her husband and children were murdered in an anti-Jewish massacre. In 1278, Rabbi Isaac Males of Toulouse was burned by the Inquisition on charges of proselytizing.

Outside Europe, conversion was even rarer. The seventh century saw the rapid rise of Islam, which spread from Spain as far as India within one hundred years. At first, Muslims treated the Jews with tolerance as "people of the book" and monotheists. But by 900, various restrictions were placed upon the thriving Jewish communities of the Islamic world. Conversion from Islam to Judaism was outlawed, and there are few recorded cases of it.

In the early Middle Ages, however, the practice of converting slaves in the Middle East, where slavery was still common, did continue. Slaves were encouraged to convert, and while the rabbis of the period refused to consider the forced conversion of slaves binding, children born to Jewish men and converted slaves were regarded as full proselytes.[22]

According to Jewish legend, there was a mass conversion during the eighth century. The story is told of Bulan, king of Khazaria (present-day Ukraine), who convened a religious debate on the relative merits of Judaism, Christianity, and Islam. Bulam decided in favor of Judaism, and he and his entire household converted. The historical record is a bit more complicated: Bulam's choice may have been politically motivated, since it freed him from paying tribute either to the Muslim caliphs or the Christian emperor.

The story of Bulam aside, conversions usually put Jewish communities at risk. Fearing reprisals and hoping to prevent violence, some rabbis enacted ordinances forbidding the acceptance of any converts. Based on midrashic commentaries on the Book of Ruth, the thirteenth-century rabbi Gershom ben Jacob decreed that converts be rebuffed three times. "Three times he is to be denied," wrote ben Jacob, but added, "In the end, he is to be accepted."[23]

Moses Maimonides, the twelfth-century rabbi, was ambivalent on the question of converts, yet he, too, ultimately sided with the proselyte. Responding to a letter from a convert named Obadiah, who asked whether he could recite certain prayers that referred to the "God of our ancestors," Maimonides answered with a resounding yes:

> In the same way as every Jew by birth says his blessing and prayer, you, too, shall bless and pray alike, whether you are alone or pray in the congregation. The reason for this is that Abraham our Father taught the people and opened minds, and revealed to them the true faith and the unity of God. . . . Ever since then whoever adopts Judaism and confesses the unity of the Divine Name, as it is prescribed in the Torah, is counted among the disciples of Abraham our Father, peace be with him. . . .
>
> There is no difference whatever between you and us. You shall certainly say the blessing: "Who has chosen us; Who

has given us; Who has taken us for Your own," and "Who has separated us." For the Creator, may He be extolled, has indeed chosen you and separated you from the nations and has given you the Torah. For the Torah has been given to us and to proselytes.[24]

The fifteenth and sixteenth centuries may have been the lowest points in the history of Jewish conversion. This was a period of social and spiritual isolation, when Jews were probably more ethnically distinctive than at any time before or since. In Europe and in the Middle East, persecution forced the Jewish community inward and inspired virulent suspicion of all outsiders. Non-Jews came to be seen as enemies, and Jews felt little enthusiasm for embracing people who seemed intent on destroying them.

Despite suspicion and danger, however, Jewish law always made a place for the convert. For centuries, editions of the *Shulchan Aruch*,[25] a popular and practical guide to Jewish law, contained a disclaimer noting that the regulations concerning conversion applied only where the civil authorities permitted Jews to accept converts. But the very existence of a chapter about converts indicates that conversion never stopped being part of Jewish life.[26]

The Enlightenment in the eighteenth century brought greater religious toleration to much of Europe. Jews in Western Europe were less persecuted and ghettoized, were permitted to study at universities, and were granted citizenship in many nations. Nevertheless, Jews and Christians lived in separate social worlds and the suspicion born of past oppression could not be forgotten. Conversion to Judaism was not common, nor was it encouraged. Moses Mendelssohn (1729–1786), a leader of the German Jewish community and a man of the secular world, summed up attitudes toward conversion, saying, "According to the principles of my faith, I must not seek to convert anyone not born a Jew. . . . My father's faith does not ask to be propagated."

The Modern Era: Nineteenth Century to the Present

AS THE MODERN ERA BEGAN, religious toleration became the official—though rarely practiced—ideology of Western civilization. Quotas and restrictions maintained the social distance between Jews and non-Jews. The term "anti-Semitism" was coined in 1897 in Germany, and anti-Jewish prejudice acquired a pseudoscientific patina, casting the Jews as an inferior race.

Many middle-class, educated Jews converted to Christianity in the 1800s—including Moses Mendelssohn's own children. However, most Jews maintained their distance from their gentile neighbors and tended to socialize with, and certainly married from within, their own community. Distrust of non-Jews was common, and even long after the secular laws against "Judaizing" had been abolished, rabbis campaigned against the idea of proselytizing. Nathan Adler, chief rabbi of the British Empire, forbade conversions in Australia without his express consent; in 1874, Adler wrote: "In principle I am very much opposed to making Jewish proselytes." In 1928, the Syrian Jewish community in Argentina decided not to accept any converts whatsoever—a decision that was supported by the chief rabbi of Palestine, Abraham Isaac Kook. As late as 1956, rabbis at a public forum in Israel charged that the ready acceptance of converts would threaten the integrity of Jewish life.[27]

However, as in all previous generations, determined individuals found a way. The most notorious example of his day was Warder Cresson, a Philadelphia Quaker who was inspired to convert during his tenure as United States consul in Jerusalem, during the 1840s. His family claimed that Cresson had lost his mind, and the ensuing sanity hearing made national headlines. Cresson was ultimately declared sane. His American wife divorced him and he returned to Jerusalem, where he married a Jew, lived out the remainder of his days, and was buried on the Mount of Olives.

Although most of the Jewish community was indifferent to conversion in the nineteenth century, some leaders of the early Reform movement tried to make Judaism more attractive to non-Jews. Traditionalists argued that the Reformers removed all impetus for formal conversion by emphasizing the universalistic elements of Jewish teachings, such as ethics and the call for social justice, and minimizing the distinctive aspects of Judaism, including the use of Hebrew and many holiday and ritual observances. Nevertheless, some Reform rabbis who made a point of welcoming converts did find an audience. Indeed, conversion was so commonplace at the Baltimore synagogue of Rabbi David Einhorn (1809–1879) that a service of acceptance was part of the prayer book there.[28]

The twentieth century saw at least three efforts to "missionize" on behalf of Judaism. The founding of the United Israel World Union (1944), the World Union for the Propagation of Judaism (1955), and the Jewish Information Society of America (1962) was announced with great fanfare. But neither Jewish theology nor history provided any basis for active proselytizing, and all three groups disappeared quickly.

Conversion became a topic of polite conversation only in the 1970s, with the coming-of-age of the Jewish baby boom. After the Second World War, American Jews were included in the life of a secular nation as never before. Restrictions were lifted, quotas were dropped, and Jews and non-Jews lived in the same neighborhoods, worked in the same corporations, hospitals, and offices, played in the same parks, and sent their children to the same schools. Jews and non-Jews saw that they shared important common values and beliefs about democracy, freedom, hard work, education, and family. Indeed, there was little to differentiate them. Liberal Jewish practice looked a great deal like Christian observance—it was less a way of life than a once-a-week (or twice-a-year) commitment. Although Jews continued to prize their ethnicity, much of it had moved into the American mainstream, which flowed with bagels and lox and knew the meaning of *chutzpah, shlemiel, shlep,* and *maven.*

Given the absence of boundaries and an increasingly shared culture, marriage between a Jew and a non-Jew no longer seemed like an alliance between different worlds. Children who had been taught to think of themselves as Americans first and Jews second and who had—for the most part—

experienced and learned little of Jewish tradition, had a difficult time understanding the parental uproar over their non-Jewish fiancées and fiancés.

Young Jews in love with non-Jews failed to realize that to their parents—even as assimilated as they were—marriage to a non-Jew represented a rejection of everything Jewish. Studies showed that the children of interfaith families rarely identify as Jews. Nobody considered conversion much of an option, and the celebrity converts of the 1950s and 1960s—Debbie Reynolds and then Liz Taylor, both prior to marrying Eddie Fisher; Marilyn Monroe before marrying Arthur Miller—tended to bolster the widely held opinion of conversion as little more than a hollow, *pro forma* gesture of appeasement.

In the early 1960s, about 9 percent of Jewish marriages were to non-Jews. Although, in retrospect, that number seems negligible, it represented such a marked increase that dire predictions about the imminent demise of the Jewish people made the cover of *Look* magazine. By the mid-seventies, when 25 percent of marriages by Jews were to non-Jews, Rabbi Alexander Schindler, president of the Union of American Hebrew Congregations, challenged the Reform movement to begin welcoming the "unchurched," especially non-Jewish spouses of Jews. An Outreach Commission was established, which set up regional and synagogue-based programs to teach non-Jews about Judaism, to encourage Jewish family formation among interfaith couples, and to instruct and welcome converts. The Conservative movement followed suit several years later.

Though the door is now open and converts are welcomed, conversion has not become a major trend. The 1990 National Jewish Population Survey showed a 52 percent rate of intermarriage, with only a small percentage—perhaps 6 percent—prompting or resulting in conversion at the time of marriage.[29] Still, even by fairly conservative estimates, as many as one out of every thirty-seven Jews in America was born to non-Jewish parents.[30] And every year, a few thousand more people convert to Judaism.

Indeed, there is now a critical mass of converts in the liberal Jewish community. Nearly all Jews know someone who chose Judaism, and most Jewish families include at least one Jew-by-choice. And it's not simply a matter of numbers. Jews-by-choice not only fill pews and classrooms, they serve as rabbis and cantors, teach in Jewish schools, and provide leadership in synagogues and other Jewish organizations.

The enthusiasm, knowledge, and commitment of converts has always been a secret source of vitality for the Jewish world. Today, however, there is no need for secrecy. Jews-by-choice are an increasingly visible and proud inspiration to the entire house of Israel.

Afterword
Kavod Ha-Ger:
Honoring the Convert

FOR NEARLY TWO THOUSAND YEARS, THE JEWISH world has treated religious seekers with polite suspicion. Ever since the first Roman edicts limiting conversion to Judaism (around 200 C.E.), converts were viewed with a mixture of curiosity and fear. The rabbis insisted upon respect for the sincere stranger (the literal translation of *ger*)—honoring him or her with the name *ger tzedek* (righteous proselyte). But the *ger*ness, the otherness, of converts actually grew over time as the gulf between Jews and non-Jews widened. As ghetto walls were fortified and *shtetl*s flourished, Jews and non-Jews ate different foods, spoke different languages, wore different clothes, studied different books, and ultimately came to doubt one another's humanity. And yet in every generation, some of the "others" expressed a desire to enter the house of Israel, confusing the Jews within. And while there was no welcome mat, the door was never barred.

There was good reason for caution in the past. The risk for converts and the Jewish community was often grave since Christian authorities sometimes executed proselytes for the crime of apostasy and Jews for the offense of accepting them. Fear poisoned the Jewish community's attitude toward converts. Thus, the rabbis' prohibition against mentioning a proselyte's non-Jewish past was meant not to shield him or her from embarrassment but to prevent Jews from being hateful. Traditional sources record explicit outrage about the way converts were treated: "You must not remind the proselyte of his pork-eating, idol-worshipping past. . . . Such verbal mockery is worse than dishonesty in business. It is comparable to the worship of idols."[1] In a deeply divided world where differences were feared and the Jewish community was closed and insular, the rabbis made the compassionate choice between spitefulness and silence. In those times, honoring the proselyte required circumspection—even to the point of secrecy.

The world that justified such a choice has vanished. In the Diaspora, the gulf between Jews and non-Jews has nearly vanished. Apart from some Orthodox enclaves, Jews and non-Jews live in the same neighborhoods, work in the same offices and hospitals, send their children to the same schools, and share many core values and beliefs. We Jews teach our children to celebrate diversity, not to fear it. Liberal Jews in particular consider Jewish pluralism a source of strength and resiliency.

And yet, when a convert seeks entrance to the Jewish community, our welcome remains nearly as muted as in the days when non-Jews seemed as alien as Martians and conversion posed a danger to anyone who so much as mentioned it. We continue to treat conversion the way we used to treat adoption.

A generation ago, adoption was a closely guarded family secret. Although there was never anything shameful or aberrant about loving and raising a child who was not born to you, adoption seemed like an admission of some kind of personal failure. Today, of course, adoption is viewed as an honorable and holy way for people to complete their families, and synagogue bulletins list adoptions by members of the congregation right next to news of births.

So where are the conversion announcements? Conversion is a normative part of Jewish life. It is, as it has always been, one of the ways that God makes more Jews. Today, conversion is more common than at any time since the beginning of the Common Era. More and more Jewish families proudly count Jews-by-choice among their nearest and dearest. Converts are members and leaders of synagogues and other Jewish organizations. Jews-by-choice are embedded in the mosaic of American Jewish life, which would not be as vital as it is without them.

In some congregations, revealing that you are a Jew-by-choice is greeted by no more (and no less) curiosity than if you said you were a South African Jew, or a Russian Jew. After all, we all come from someplace. We are all hyphenated. We all introduce ourselves with a variety of adjectives and modifiers:

Reconstructionist Jew, Jewish feminist, California Jew, child of survivors, Israeli Jew, secular Jew, rural Jew. In this context, discovering that someone is a Jew-by-choice is nothing more or less than a salient detail, a pleasant surprise, and, increasingly, a point of honor.

Some congregations do list conversions in the temple bulletin and announce them from the *bimah*—along with news of engagements and weddings, births and adoptions. And in some synagogues, new Jews are given *aliyot* and publicly acclaimed by rabbis beaming with affection and pride. Converts are invited to tell their stories at adult education programs and to students in the religious school. Rabbis preach about the positive contributions made by converts and single out Jews-by-choice for particular honors. One rabbi honors the converts of his congregation on the busiest day of the Jewish year: "On Rosh Hashanah morning, when it comes time for the reading of the Akeda, I tell the congregation that Abraham not only figures in the Akeda story but was also the first person to bring others under the wings of *Shechinah*. Since there are many people in the congregation who chose to become Jews as adults, it seems appropriate to call upon someone who has chosen to be a Jew as we turn to a Torah reading about Abraham. A Jew-by-choice does the first *aliyah* on behalf of all other converts in the congregation. The feeling in the sanctuary at that moment is electric."[2]

Jews-by-choice report that the response to such forms of congregational recognition is overwhelmingly positive and deeply moving. Strangers and friends approach with handshakes, hugs, and congratulations. But the impact on the born-Jewish members of the congregation is just as powerful. For a people whose history has left deep psychological scars, the sight of a bright, thoughtful person voluntarily embracing Judaism is an antidote to Jewish ambivalence, which was given its most succinct form in Groucho Marx's famous wisecrack, "I wouldn't want to belong to any club that would accept me as a member."

Jews-by-choice are, by their very existence, messengers and teachers whose presence reminds the community that Judaism is an open religious culture. That neither Abraham nor Sarah were born to Jewish mothers. That Ruth is not a quaint biblical tale but an ongoing story of creation. That in the world today, being Jewish is not a label but an avocation—a choice.

And yet, the old maxim remains true: it's not easy to be a Jew. Any kind of Jew.

While few born-Jews view non-Jews as wholly "other" anymore, conversion still poses a challenge. Although converts don't invite physical threats to the community, they do raise fundamental questions about what it means to be a Jew, about why a person would choose to be Jewish at all. And those are questions that make lots of Jews squirm—especially Jews for whom Judaism is a passive, ethnic identity rather than a living practice.

Jews-by-choice often answer the questions they raise in the ways that they embrace traditions and practices and reasons for being Jewish that many born-Jews have forgotten or dismissed. Jews-by-choice become Jews for a hundred good reasons, spoken without apology or hesitation. "Because the Torah speaks to me." "Because *mitzvot* give meaning to my daily life." "Because I wish to be part of a tradition that sees working for justice as a religious imperative." "Because this is a religious identity I want to give to my children." "Because when I light Shabbat candles, I feel God's presence around me."

The paradigms of Jewish life have shifted. Virtually all Jews have non-Jewish relatives, and quite soon literally all Jews will be related to a Jew-by-choice. So how do we show respect for our new sisters and brothers? What is the proper expression of *kavod ha-ger* for four thousand new Jews every year?

The old choice no longer works; it is no longer a matter of rejection or silence. The real choice today is between gossipy whispers (when were Jews ever really silent about the *yichus* of their brethren?) and outspoken welcome. The choice is between "politely" ignoring the convert's path and celebrating and learning from his or her journey.

Jews-by-choice enrich the Jewish community in countless ways. Rabbis who work with converts are inspired and energized by their students' sincerity, integrity, and love of Judaism. Converts pour their enthusiasm into synagogues and Jewish organizations. And Jews-by-choice give the Jewish community the opportunity to bring more holiness into the world by providing the opportunity to perform the *mitzvot* of *hachnasat ha-ger* and *kavod ha-ger*.

As *mitzvot*—not resolutions or platform statements— *hachnasat ha-ger* and *kavod ha-ger* enjoin us to act, both as individuals and as communities; to do everything in our power to embrace Jews-by-choice. To create mentoring programs and support groups for recent converts. To foster sensitivity to community diversity so that people stop making stupid remarks about who looks Jewish and who doesn't. To improve training for rabbis, cantors, and educators around issues of conversion. To make conversion rituals memorable and beautiful. To teach the history of conversion. To provide ever better adult education opportunities for all Jews. To put out the welcome mat and open the door.

Resources

The Movements

Conservative

The Conservative movement does not coordinate conversion programs on a national basis. Rabbis in various geographic regions offer courses and oversee conversions.

Speak to a local Conservative rabbi about how to connect with the conversion programs in your area, or contact the Rabbinical Assembly, 3080 Broadway, New York, NY 10027 (212-280-6000).

The Rabbinical Assembly, the professional association of Conservative rabbis, welcomes inquiries from potential converts and can provide referrals. You can e-mail them from their Website, www.rabassembly.org.

Reconstructionist

The Reconstructionist movement offers a thirty-week introductory course to Judaism called "Jewish, Alive, and American." This class may, with the sponsorship of a local rabbi, be used for formal conversion studies.

To find a Reconstructionist congregation in your area, contact the Jewish Reconstructionist Federation, 1299 Church Road, Wyncote, PA 19095 (215-887-1988).

Reform

Of the liberal movements, Reform offers the most comprehensive national program under the title of "Outreach." It publishes a variety of materials and sponsors conversion courses and support groups throughout North America.

Any Reform temple can refer you to the regional office nearest you, or check local listings for the Union of American Hebrew Congregations—the official name of Reform Judaism. You can also contact the national headquarters of Reform Jewish Outreach at the UAHC, 838 Fifth Avenue, New York, NY 10021 (212-650-4230; http://shamash.org/reform/uahc/outreach).

Nondenominational Resources

Derekh Torah: The Way of Torah

Offered by Jewish community centers in several cities around the United States, this twenty-week introductory course is for individuals and couples who wish to explore Judaism and define its place in their lives through study of theology, history, and practice. While this is not a conversion class, it provides an excellent overview and its teachers can provide referrals to local rabbis who do supervise conversions.

For information about Derekh Torah in your community, contact the local Jewish community center. Or get in touch with the Jewish Community Centers Association, 15 East 26th Street, New York, NY 10010 (212-532-4949).

In greater New York City, call the Bronfman Center for Jewish Life at the 92nd Street Y, 1395 Lexington Avenue, New York, NY 10128 (212-415-5767; http://www.92ndsty.org).

Jewish Converts Network

A private, nonprofit, nonsectarian network of local support groups for new and prospective converts. The group's founder, Lena Romanoff, trains facilitators who help new Jews learn more about Judaism and make connections in the community. "No one should go through conversion alone," says Romanoff, a Jew-by-choice. The Jewish Converts Network can help you find existing support groups or assist you in establishing one in your community.

For information, write or call: 1112 Hagy's Ford Road, Narberth, PA 19072 (610-664-8112).

Stars of David

Stars of David International, Inc., is a nonprofit, national support network for Jewish adoptive parents. (Note: This is *not* an adoption agency.) Stars of David has active chapters in cities around the country, and a membership that includes Jews of all affiliations, interfaith couples, single parents, prospective parents, transracial couples, those with biological children, and grandparents.

To find out more, call 800-STAR349 or contact Susan M. Katz at 3175 Commercial Avenue, Suite 100, Northbrook, IL 60062-1915 (847-509-9929; http://www.webassist.com/stars-of-david/).

Converts and Conversion

A Bibliography

Guidebooks and Advice

Conversion to Judaism: A Guidebook by Lawrence J. Epstein. Jason Aronson, 1994. An overview of the subject, including some dramatic stories of conversion, a brief history, and basic information about the rituals and emotional processes associated with becoming a Jew. The book also includes "A Basic Guide" to Judaism itself, including discussions of Jewish beliefs, texts, history, and practices.

Becoming Jewish: A Handbook for Conversion by Rabbi Ronald H. Isaacs. Rabbinical Assembly, 1993. A very brief introduction (39 pages) to some of the issues of conversion. Most of this short volume provides a guide to Jewish holidays and home rituals. Published by the Conservative movement.

Choosing Judaism by Lydia Kukoff. Union of American Hebrew Congregations, 1981. Kukoff broke ground with her book. Written in the first person by a Jew-by-choice for others considering conversion, it's a friendly, down-to-earth introduction to interpersonal issues. Published by the Reform movement.

Becoming a Jew by Rabbi Maurice Lamm. Jonathan David Publishers, 1991. *The* Orthodox guide to conversion; comprehensive and remarkably welcoming. Rabbi Lamm includes a section on legal (halachic) questions concerning conversion and converts, and an overview of Orthodox Jewish belief and practice.

The Intermarriage Handbook: A Guide for Jews and Christians by Judy Petsonk and Jim Remsen. William Morrow, 1988. Thoughtful, sensitive, and comprehensive, this book, though intended for interfaith couples and families, is very useful for converts. In addition to an excellent chapter on conversion, you'll find tips on dealing with ethnic differences within a marriage, and good ideas about coping with families of origin.

Your People, My People: Finding Acceptance and Fulfillment as a Jew by Choice by Lena Romanoff with Lisa Hostein. Jewish Publication Society, 1990. Ms. Romanoff is a convert who speaks from her own experience. She also quotes many other Jews-by-choice about the process of becoming Jewish. Full of important information, insights, and useful ideas for the Jewish community and the rabbinate as well as for converts.

First-Person Accounts

Embracing the Covenant: Converts to Judaism Talk About Why, edited by Rabbi Allan Berkowitz and Patti Moskovitz. Jewish Lights Publishing, 1996. Twenty Jews-by-choice speak (and some write poetry) about what inspired them to become Jewish.

So Strange My Path by Abraham Carmel. Bloch Publishing Co., 1964. The story of a religious seeker who was, for a time, a Roman Catholic priest. Carmel, a Scotsman, wrote this volume seven years after his conversion to what he refers to as "the Mother Faith."

San Nicandro: The Story of a Religious Phenomenon by Elena Cassin, translated by Douglas West. Dufour Editions, 1962. An unusual story of a Christian who found his way, through visions and identification with biblical ideals, to Judaism, and then brought a whole Italian community with him to Israel.

Stranger in the Midst: A Memoir of Spiritual Discovery by Nan Fink. A complicated, sometimes painful contemporary conversion story. Basic Books, 1997.

In This Dark House by Louise Kehoe. Schocken Books, 1995. This is not a "conversion story" per se, but a beautifully written account of a difficult childhood, which begins to make sense only when the author discovers that her father was a Jew. Conversion is part of a personal journey toward healing.

Lovesong: Becoming a Jew by Julius Lester. Henry Holt and Co., 1988. A passionate and fascinating account of how an African-American writer—the great-grandson of a Jew—satisfies his soul's longing in Judaism.

Finding a Home for the Soul, edited by Catherine Hall Myrowitz. Jason Aronson, 1995. This collection of forty-three interviews illustrates the variety of people who choose Judaism: male and female, gay and straight, black and white. Jews of all stripes are included in the book, despite a decidedly traditional/ Orthodox bias.

Pilgrimage of a Proselyte: From Auschwitz to Jerusalem by David Patterson. Jonathan David Publishers, 1993. This is a diary of a two-week journey from Patterson's home in the United States to the death camps of Poland, to the land of Israel, and back to the United States.

The Bamboo Cradle: A Jewish Father's Story by Avraham Schwartzbaum. Feldheim Publishers, 1989. While a Fulbright scholar in Taiwan, Schwartzbaum found a newborn baby who had been abandoned in a train station. He and his wife adopted her, and their decision, four years later, to have Hsin-Mei/Devorah converted began the Schwartzbaum's journey into Orthodox Judaism.

Hope Is My House by Deborah Wigoder. Prentice-Hall, 1966. The story of how Jane Frances MacDwyer, a Catholic Irish-American, becomes Deborah Emmit Jaffe Wigoder, a Jew living in the infant state of Israel. A unique slice of history.

Fiction

Mona in the Promised Land by Gish Jen. Knopf, 1996. Chinese-American high school girl converts to Judaism. Funny and wise.

The Assistant by Bernard Malamud. Farrar, Straus and Cudahy, 1957. In Malamud's second novel, the non-Jewish assistant to a poverty-stricken Jewish grocer falls in love with his boss's daughter.

The Slave (in *Three Complete Novels*) by Isaac Bashevis Singer. Avenel Books, 1982. The story of a Polish Jew, enslaved during the dark days of the pogroms, who falls in love with his master's beautiful daughter.

For children:

King of the Seventh Grade by Barbara Cohen. Lothrop, Lee and Shepard, 1989. Vic hates Hebrew school and wants no part of his bar mitzvah—until he's told he can't have one because his mother isn't Jewish. Vic's decision to formally convert is part of this coming-of-age story. Grades 6 and up.

Mommy Never Went to Hebrew School by Mindy Portnoy. Kar-Ben, 1989. The story of a parent's conversion, for very young children.

History of Conversion

Conversion to Judaism: A History and an Analysis, edited by David Max Eichhorn. Ktav, 1965. A collection of essays by several rabbis on specific periods in history and such areas of inquiry as the sociology and theology of conversion.

The Theory and Practice of Welcoming Converts to Judaism by Lawrence J. Epstein. Dyfed, Wales: Edwin Mellen Press, 1992. Epstein makes a strong case for Judaism's fundamental openness to converts, supported by interesting historical and rabbinic materials.

The Conversion Crisis: Essays from the Pages of "Tradition" Magazine, edited by Emanuel Feldman and Joel B. Wolowelsky. Ktav, 1990. A look at the Orthodox community's views on what is seen as a "crisis" created by intermarriage and non-Orthodox conversions. In his essay "Another Halakhic Approach to Conversions," Rabbi Marc Angel articulates the most welcoming point of view in this collection, arguing that "there is no requirement to ask the non-Jew actually to observe the *mitzvot*" and that conversion is itself a *mitzvah*. Published by the Orthodox movement.

Jews by Choice: A Study of Converts to Reform and Conservative Judaism by Brenda Forster and Rabbi Joseph Tabachnik. Ktav, 1991. A study by a sociologist and a Conservative rabbi conducted in Chicago in 1987–88. Interesting findings and observations, though the use of the term "conversionary intermarriage" is unfortunate.

Conversion to Judaism: From the Biblical Period to the Present by Joseph R. Rosenbloom. Hebrew Union College Press, 1978. Lots of interesting information that suggest how much is yet to be written on the subject—from dissertations to novels.

Glossary

alef-bet—name of the Hebrew alphabet; also, its first two letters.

aliyah—literally, "to go up." In the synagogue, to be called to the Torah. "Making *aliyah*" refers to moving to the land of Israel.

Apocrypha—fourteen "writings," including the Book of Esther, that were not included in the final version of the Bible, but which are, nevertheless, important Jewish texts.

Aramaic—ancient Semitic language closely related to Hebrew. The Talmud was written in Aramaic.

Ashkenazim—Jews and Jewish culture of Eastern and Central Europe.

aufruf—literally, "called up." Recognition given when people are called up to the Torah on Shabbat, typically before a wedding.

Baal Shem Tov—Israel ben Eliezer, the founder of Hasidism, the eighteenth-century mystical revival movement.

Baruch ata Adonai—words that begin Hebrew blessings, most commonly rendered in English as "Blessed art Thou, Lord our God, King of the Universe." This book contains a number of alternatives to that translation.

bat—daughter, or daughter of; as in bat mitzvah, daughter of the commandment. Pronounced "baht."

B.C.E.—before the Common Era. Jews avoid the Christian designation B.C., which means "before Christ."

bet din—a court (literally, a "house of judgment") of three rabbis that is convened to witness and give communal sanction to events such as conversions to Judaism.

bris—Yiddish for *brit,* the most common way of referring to the covenant of circumcision.

brit—covenant.

brit milah—the covenant of circumcision.

bubbe—Yiddish word for "grandma."

C.E.—Common Era. Jews avoid A.D., which stands for *anno domini,* or "in the year of our Lord."

cantor—leader of synagogue services trained in Jewish liturgical music.

challah—braided loaf of egg bread, traditional for Shabbat, the holidays, and other festive occasions.

chutzpah—courage, nerve, brass.

Conservative Judaism—a religious movement developed in the United States during the twentieth century as a more traditional response to modernity than that offered by Reform Judaism.

daven—pray.

Diaspora—exile. The dwelling of Jews outside the Holy Land.

d'rash—religious insight, often on a text from the Torah. *D'rashot* is the plural.

d'var Torah—literally, "words of Torah"; an explication of a portion of the Torah.

dreidel—a top used for playing a child's game of chance during the festival of Hanukkah.

erev—"the evening before" the day. Jewish days begin at sunset, not sunrise.

flayshig—meat food, which according to *kashrut*, or traditional laws governing what Jews eat, may not be mixed with dairy products.

ger—proselyte, convert, stranger. *Giyoret* is the feminine. *Giur* is the process of conversion.

Haggadah—the book containing the liturgy of the Passover seder.

haimish—Yiddish for homelike; giving one a sense of belonging.

halachah—traditional Jewish law, contained in the Talmud and its commentaries.

Hasidism—eighteenth-century mystical revival, a movement that stressed God's presence in the world and the idea that joy could be seen as a way of communing with God.

havdalah—separation. The Saturday evening ceremony that separates Shabbat from the rest of the week.

havurah—fellowship. A small, self-directed group that meets for prayer, study, and celebration.

hazzan—cantor. *Hazzanit* is the feminine form.

huppah—wedding canopy.

kashrut—traditional system of laws governing what and how Jews eat.

ketubah—marriage contract.

kiddush—sanctification; also the blessing over wine.

klezmer—a joyful, soulful form of Jewish music that blends military marches, European folk songs, dance tunes, and American jazz.

kohane—the biblical social class that comprised the priesthood.

kosher—foods deemed fit for consumption according to the laws of *kashrut*.

maven—an expert.

mazel tov—literally, "Good luck." In common use, it means "Congratulations."

megillah—scroll. The Book of Esther, the text for Purim, is the Megillat Esther, usually called "the megillah." Also a Yiddish term that means "story."

mensch—person; an honorable, decent person.

mezuzah—the first two paragraphs of the Shema, a Jewish prayer, written on a parchment scroll and encased in a small container, affixed to the doorposts of a home.

midrash—imaginative exposition of stories based on the Bible.

mikvah—ritual bath.

milah—circumcision. *Brit milah* is the covenant of circumcision.

milchig—dairy foods, which, according to *kashrut*, may not be mixed with meat.

minhag—custom.

minyan—a prayer quorum of ten adult Jews. For traditional Jews, ten men.

Mishnah—the first part of the Talmud, composed of six "orders" of laws regarding everything from agriculture to marriage.

mishpachah— Hebrew and Yiddish for "family."

mitzvah—a sacred obligation or commandment, mentioned in the Torah.

mohel—one who is trained in the rituals and procedures of *brit milah*, circumcision. Pronounced "mo-*hail*," in Hebrew; "moil" in Yiddish.

motzi—blessing over bread recited before meals.

nachas—special joy from the achievements of one's children.

niggun—a wordless, prayerlike melody.

oneg Shabbat—literally, "joy of the Sabbath." A gathering, for food and fellowship, after Friday night synagogue services.

Orthodox Judaism—the modern Orthodox movement developed in the nineteenth century in response to the Enlightenment and Reform Judaism.

parasha—the weekly Torah portion.

Pesach—Passover.

pogrom—a massacre of Jews.

rabbi—teacher. A rabbi is a seminary-ordained member of the clergy. "The rabbis" refers to the men who codified the Talmud.

Reconstructionist Judaism—a religious movement begun in the United States in the twentieth century by Mordecai Kaplan, who saw Judaism as an evolving religious civilization.

Reform Judaism—a movement begun in nineteenth-century Germany that sought to reconcile Jewish tradition with modernity and does not accept the divine authority of *halachah.*

Rosh Hodesh—the first day of every lunar month; the New Month, a semiholiday.

sandek—Jewish godfather; the one who holds the baby during a circumcision. *Sandeket* is a new term for Jewish godmother.

s'eudat mitzvah—a commanded meal; the festive celebration of a milestone. Plural: *s'eudot mitzvah.*

Shabbat—Sabbath. In Yiddish, Shabbos.

Shechinah—God's feminine attributes.

shehehiyanu—a prayer of thanksgiving for new blessings.

Shema—the Jewish prayer that declares God's unity.

sheva brachot—the seven marriage blessings.

shidduch—match; as in "a match made in heaven."

shlemiel—a simpleton, a fall guy, a clumsy oaf.

shlep—to carry, drag around.

shofar—ram's horn, sounded during the High Holidays.

shtetl—a small Eastern European town inhabited by Ashkenazic Jews before the Holocaust.

shul—synagogue.

siddur—prayer book.

simcha—joy and the celebration of joy.

taharat hamishpachah—laws of family purity prescribing women's sexual availability and the use of *mikvah*.

tallis, tallit—prayer shawl. *Tallis* is Yiddish, *tallit* is Hebrew.

Talmud—collection of rabbinic thought and laws, 200 B.C.E. to 500 C.E.

Tanach—the book that contains the entire Hebrew Bible, including the Torah, the Writings, and the Prophets.

tikkun olam—repairing the world. A fundamental Jewish concept of taking responsibility for improving the temporal world.

Torah—the first five books of the Hebrew Bible, divided into fifty-four portions that are read aloud and studied in an annual cycle. For some Jews, the Torah contains the literal word of God. For liberal Jews, however, and for the purposes of this book, the Torah is a human record of an encounter with the holy.

tzedakah—righteous giving or action on behalf of the poor; charity.

yichus—family status. Pride in family members' achievements.

Yiddish—language spoken by Ashkenazic Jews, a combination of early German and Hebrew.

Yom Kippur—Day of Atonement, the holiest of the High Holidays.

Notes

INTRODUCTION: The Journey to Judaism

1. The denominations (Reform, Conservative, Reconstructionist, modern Orthodox) do not keep conversion statistics. There is no registry for Jews-by-choice, and no one has launched a careful study of the subject. The figure cited here originates with Professor Egon Mayer, a sociologist with the Graduate Center of the City University of New York and coauthor of the National Jewish Population Survey of 1990. An earlier figure of ten thousand converts to Judaism per year also originated with Dr. Mayer; but as of 1995, Mayer said that number was far too high.

2. Lawrence J. Epstein, *Conversion to Judaism: A Guidebook* (Northvale, N.J.: Jason Aronson, 1994), p. 38.

3. For a thorough and readable introduction to the religious beliefs of liberal Jews, see *Liberal Judaism* by Eugene Borowitz (New York: Union of American Hebrew Congregations, 1984).

PART I: Making Your Way

New Definitions

1. Julius Lester, *Lovesong: Becoming a Jew* (New York: Henry Holt and Co., 1988).

2. Rabbi Barbara Penzner calls this a "horizontal identification, as opposed to the vertical identification, of history."

3. The differences between the movements are elaborated throughout this book, with the caveat that there are substantial differences among rabbis within the same movement. For example, the Conservative movement and all Conservative rabbis require immersion and circumcision of converts. The Reform movement's position is that these rituals are "optional," but individual Reform rabbis may well require them of students for conversion.

4. In *Becoming a Jew*, Maurice Lamm's book on Orthodox conversion, Moses Maimonides' (1135–1204) "Thirteen Articles of Faith" are cited as "fundamental principles which are axiomatic and considered critical to right belief." These include: "Belief that the Torah was given by God to Moses. Belief that the Torah is immutable. Belief that God knows the thoughts and deeds of men. Belief that God rewards and punishes. Belief in the advent of the Messiah. Belief in the resurrection of the dead" ([Middle Village, N.Y.: Jonathan David Publishers, 1991], pp. 278–79).

   In terms of religious observance, Orthodox conversion entails a promise to: maintain a strictly kosher home, scrupulously observe the Sabbath, obey the laws of family purity (*taharat hamishpachah*) which regulate sexual activity, and send your children to Orthodox Jewish schools.

5. One source for the discouraging of converts is this text: "Three times he is to be denied," wrote Rabbi Gershom ben Jacob, a thirteenth-century German rabbi, adding, "In the end, he is to be accepted." See Part VI, "Your History: A Short History of Conversion to Judaism."

6. In fact, this is a problem for all immigrants who wish to marry in Israel. Immigrants must provide proof that their mothers were born Jewish or that their conversions were done under Orthodox auspices. Converts and immigrants find ways around the law. Many go to Cyprus for a wedding that the Israeli government will then recognize. Russian immigrants in Israel face the same difficulties. Legal experts predict that the large number of Russians will eventually cause a change in the laws.

   Thanks to Brian Rosman for exploring and explaining the complexities of the situation in Israel, which is fluid.

7. For a longer discussion of this subject, see the chapter "Are the Jews

Chosen?" in *Liberal Judaism* by Eugene Borowitz (New York: Union of American Hebrew Congregations, 1984), pp. 52–67.

8.   Abraham Joshua Heschel, *God in Search of Man: A Philosophy of Judaism* (New York: Farrar, Straus and Giroux, 1955), p. 425.

9.   Mechilta Bachodesh 5.

10.   From a speech on the occasion of the author's conversion to Judaism at Fairmount Temple, Anshe Chesed Congregation, Cleveland, Ohio, 1994.

11.   Yevamot 47a.

12.   From a sermon delivered by Rabbi Samuel Chiel, Temple Emanuel, Newton Centre, Massachusetts, September 1992.

13.   A small minority of Orthodox Jews opposed the creation of a state as impious, arguing that only God could restore Israel, as promised in the Bible.

Family Matters

Special thanks to Dr. Judith Himber, June Horowitz, Rabbi Elaine Zecher, Kathy Kahn, and Susan Kasanof, whose insights inform this chapter.

14.   See Judy Petsonk and Jim Remsen, "Dealing with Parents: Push and Pull," in *The Intermarriage Handbook: A Guide for Jews and Christians* (New York: William Morrow, 1988), pp. 39–59.

15.   From Hilary Tham, *Bad Names for Women* (Washington, D.C.: Word Works, 1992).

16.   Egon Mayer, interview with the author, 1995.

17.   According to the study by Brenda Forster and Rabbi Joseph Tabachnik of converts conducted in the late 1980s, Jews-by-choice who married born-Jews reported that 46 percent of their Jewish fathers-in-law and 47 percent of their Jewish mothers-in-law seemed "disappointed or neutral" about their child's marriage to a convert. Eighteen percent of the fathers and 14 percent of the mothers did not seem supportive of the conversion at all (*Jews by Choice: A Study of Converts to Reform and Conservative Judaism* [Hoboken, N.J.: Ktav, 1991], p. 97).

18.   According to Professor Egon Mayer, 90 percent of converts—in all religions, not just Judaism—are women. "This clearly raises the question of power and sex roles," he notes. (From an interview with the author, 1995.)

19.   Kirtland Snyder, "Diary of a Conversion," *Midstream*, August 1984.

20. Rabbi Maurice Lamm argues in favor of those who convert "for the sake of the family."

21. Joseph B. Soloveichik, "Beyn Brisk L'Boston" (From Brisk to Boston), *Hadoar,* September 5, 1986, p. 7.

22. Edwin H. Friedman, a family systems therapist and rabbi, has written extensively on the subject of Jewish family dynamics.

23. See Petsonk and Remsen, "Ethnic Background: Your Cradle Culture" and "Ethnic Ambivalence: Love that Blonde," in *The Intermarriage Handbook,* pp. 85–111.

24. From a joke that appears in *Jewish Humor: What the Best Jewish Jokes Have to Say About the Jews* by Rabbi Joseph Telushkin (New York: William Morrow, 1992), p. 140.

25. *Gilgul* is the Hebrew for "metempsychosis" or "transmigration." The idea of transmigration of souls was a common belief in the ancient world, and one shared by many Jews. Although neither the Bible nor the Talmud makes any mention of this idea, it is a folk belief that has persisted throughout Jewish history.

26. The blessings, which appear in the chapter on *mikvah,* are the same ones used by anyone using the *mikvah,* including brides, postmenstrual women, and people preparing for the High Holidays.

PART II: *Preparation*

Choosing Your Rabbi

1. Most rabbis receive little or no professional instruction about conversion during their seminary training.

2. "Hillel" is the name given to the Jewish campus "ministry" at many universities and colleges, named after one of the great teachers of Judaism, who is mentioned later in this chapter.

Study

3. Mishnah Pe'ah 1.1. Also recited in the morning prayer service.

4. It's interesting to note that there is no mention of faith or prayer or God in this list.

5. Barry Holtz, *Back to the Sources: Reading the Classic Jewish Texts* (New York: Summit Books, 1984), p. 12.

6. These particular words come from the mouth of Rabbi Lawrence Kushner.

7. This definition, and indeed much of the following discussion of *midrash*, is beholden to Rabbi Norman J. Cohen, provost of the New York School of the Hebrew Union College–Jewish Institute of Religion, where he is also Professor of Midrash.

8. Some Jewish community centers around the country offer a twenty-week nondenominational introductory course called Derekh Torah (The Path of Torah) which features small classes, is led by select and highly motivated teachers, and meets in people's homes rather than in institutions. See Resources.

9. In addition to Hebrew, there are three other languages written with the Hebrew *alef-bet* (alphabet) which are part of Jewish history and culture: Aramaic is an ancient Semitic language, the language of the Talmud, and also Jesus' spoken tongue; Yiddish, a combination of Hebrew, German, and words borrowed from other languages, is still spoken by Jews of Eastern European descent (Ashkenazim); Ladino a combination of Hebrew and Spanish, is still spoken among Jews of Mediterranean (Sephardic) background. Both Yiddish and Ladino have a rich literature that includes poetry, lyrics, prayers, and fiction.

10. For help in locating Jewish destinations, consult *The Jewish Traveler: Hadassah Magazine's Guide to the World's Jewish Communities and Sights,* ed. Alan Tigay (Northvale, N.J.: Jason Aronson, 1994).

11. Dan Wakefield *The Story of Your Life: Writing a Spiritual Autobiography* (Boston: Beacon Press, 1990), p. 42. This book is a useful resource for anyone keeping a conversion journal, and for Jewish professionals working with converts.

Choosing a Hebrew Name

12. Orthodox converts often do legally change their given names.

13. Maurice Lamm, *Becoming a Jew* (Middle Village, N.Y.: Jonathan David Publishers, 1991), p. 184.

14. Alfred J. Kolatch *The Name Dictionary* (Middle Village, N.Y.: Jonathan David Publishers, 1967), p. xi.

15. Although this custom is not found in the Bible, it is a very ancient

practice, common among the Egyptian Jews of the sixth century B.C.E., who most likely borrowed the idea from their non-Jewish neighbors. Ashkenazic Jews—those of Eastern European descent— name their children only after relatives who have passed away. Sephardim name their children after living relations.

16. In many liberal congregations, the words *avienu* and *imenu* are not used when calling someone to the Torah. Converts are simply ben or bat Avraham v'Sarah.

PART III: *Rituals and Ceremonies*

The Covenant of Circumcision

1. Yalkut Mishle, 964.
2. Maurice Lamm, *Becoming a Jew* (Middle Village, N.Y.: Jonathan David Publishers, 1991), p. 152.
3. Abraham's son, Isaac, was circumcised on the eighth day, which is why the ritual has been performed on eight-day-old babies ever since.
4. Exodus 4:24–25.
5. See *Europa Europa*, the 1991 film by Agnieszka Holland, which treats circumcision under Nazi oppression with pathos and humor.
6. For more about the traditional interpretations of circumcision, see *Bris Milah*, ed. Rabbis Nosson Scherman and Meir Zlotowitz (Brooklyn, N.Y.: Mesorah Publications, 1969).
7. According to the American Association of Pediatrics, properly performed newborn circumcision prevents a variety of rare mechanical and inflammatory problems of the penis and has been shown to decrease incidence of cancer of the penis, which is also rare. New research also suggests that the procedure may protect against infections of the kidney and urinary tract. See "Policy Report of the Task Force on Circumcision," *AAP News*, March 1989, p. 7: "Properly performed newborn circumcision prevents phimosis, paraphimosis and balanoposthitis."
8. Moses Maimonides, *Guide for the Perplexed*, translated from the Arabic by M. Friedlander (New York: Dover, 1956), p. 378.
9. Bereshit Rabbah.

10. The fact that women are not included in this core element of the covenant is a source of ancient and contemporary debate.

11. For more on the Reform decision, see "Without Milah and Tevilah" by Richard Rosenthal, in *Conversion to Judaism in Jewish Law: Essays and Responsa*, ed. Walter Jacob and Moshe Zemer (Pittsburgh: Rodef Shalom Press, 1994). Also in the same volume, "Circumcision of Proselytes."

12. In the 1960s, 95 percent of all baby boys were circumcised. In 1971, the American Academy of Pediatrics announced that there was no medical reason for surgical removal of the foreskin, and by 1985 only 59 percent of newborn boys underwent the procedure, which was no longer automatically covered by medical insurance.

13. This *kavannah* was written by Rabbi Lawrence S. Kushner.

14. Julius Lester's conversion to Judaism ultimately included adult circumcision followed by *hatafat dam brit*. In his memoir *Lovesong: Becoming a Jew*, (New York: Henry Holt and Co., 1988), Lester describes the experience in some detail.

Final Exam: The Bet Din

15. Historically, a *bet din* was comprised of three observant Jewish males; in the liberal Jewish community, women serve on liberal Jewish tribunals.

16. Lamm, *Becoming a Jew*, p. 123.

17. This question echoes Maimonides' warning statement to would-be converts: "Do you not know that our people is in a loathsome condition, oppressed, prostrate, torn, and in agony?" According to Maimonides, if a person persists in the desire to become a Jew, even after this warning, he or she is to be welcomed.

Mikvah: A River from Eden

18. As cited in Aryeh Kaplan, *Waters of Eden: The Mystery of the Mikvah*. (New York: National Conference of Synagogue Youth/Union of Orthodox Jewish Congregations of America, 1976), p. 35.

19. Christianity acknowledges the purifying, regenerative power of water in the ritual of baptism, which may have been borrowed from Jewish practice.

20. In Hebrew, *taharat hamishpachah*.

21. The increased use of *mikvah* by liberal converts has led to the building of a few Reform *mikva'ot*.

22. Exodus 19:10.

23. Exodus 12:38.

24. *Tevilah* as a precondition for sexual activity—a purification from the *niddah*, or ritual impurity of menstruation—has long offended liberal Jews. However, Orthodox women (and men) argue that the laws of family purity (*taharat hamishpachah*) are not demeaning to women, but are, in fact, spiritually sensitive to women's monthly cycles.

25. For an interesting description of a Hasidic *mikvah* in Crown Heights, read "The Mikvah" in *Holy Days: The World of a Hasidic Family* by Lis Harris (New York: Summit Books, 1985), pp. 135–49.

26. Lamm, "The Absence of Melodrama," in *Becoming a Jew*, pp. 164–66.

27. This ceremony, based on one performed by Rabbi Lawrence Kushner, includes the basic blessings with a few additional readings—some of which are used in synagogue conversion ceremonies.

Conversion Ceremonies

28. This is still true in some Reform congregations.

29. Generalizations based on movement affiliation are no longer useful. Many Reform rabbis today urge or even require *milah* and *mikvah* and offer a public ceremony as an option only. On the other hand, Conservative and Reconstructionist congregations routinely offer converts the choice of a public honor during a special Shavuot program or at a regular Shabbat Torah service—in addition to the halachic rituals, of course.

30. This honor to Jews-by-choice is something like that given to brides and grooms, who are often given a congregational "send-off" with an *aufruf*—where the affianced couple is called to the Torah for blessings and is pelted with candy.

31. Thanks to Lorel Zar-Kessler, cantor at Congregation Beth El of the Sudbury River Valley, where this version of the *mi she'beirach* is used.

32. This is one version of the kinds of questions typically asked of converts. Sometimes, these are asked by the *bet din* or at the *mikvah* instead.

33. "The rabbi put his hands on my head. The fact that he made physical

contact made it a very intimate thing—an emotional, powerful, intense feeling. I had the sense that time was passing really slowly."

34. Translation by Joan Betesh.

35. This service, which is folded into a regular Shabbat service, is also used for groups of converts. It was adapted from a ceremony developed by Rabbi Dennis C. Sasso. A version of this service appeared in *Conservative Judaism*, Summer 1984. It is printed here by permission of Rabbi Sasso, with thanks for his help and encouragement.

36. The prayers and order of *havdalah* are printed in most *siddurim*, or prayer books, and in many introductory books about Jewish practice, including *Living a Jewish Life* by Anita Diamant with Howard Cooper (New York: HarperCollins, 1991).

Conversion of Children

37. This conundrum is presented in a young adult novel called *King of the Seventh Grade*, in which the protagonist, Vic, discovers that he is not permitted to become bar mitzvah in the family's Conservative synagogue because his mother did not convert before his birth. *King of the Seventh Grade* by Barbara Cohen (New York: Lothrop, Lee and Shepard, 1982).

38. Only the first stanza refers to adoption and may be omitted if the child was born to you. The prayer itself comes from a ceremony by Rabbi Edward Treister and Rochelle Treister, Houston, Texas, June 17, 1986.

39. Janelle Bohrod, "Janelle Bohrod's Story," *Star Tracks*, Spring 1986, pp. 5–7.

40. Joseph Adolph, M.D.

41. For more on names and naming, see Anita Diamant, *The New Jewish Baby Book* (Woodstock, Vt..: Jewish Lights Publishing, 1993).

42. Orthodox Jews maintain the ben/bat Avraham v'Sara construction for children. Another old custom, rarely followed nowadays, is to add the term *ha-m'gadlo* (the one who raises him) after the adoptive father's name. However, the overwhelming custom among liberal Jews is for adopted children to take their adoptive parents' names.

43. Seong means "beauty." You can make naming decisions apparent, if you wish, on the adoption announcement. See Diamant, *The New Jewish Baby Book*, p. 198.

44. Sanhedrin 19b.
45. Lawrence J. Epstein, *The Theory and Practice of Welcoming Converts to Judaism* (Dyfed, Wales: Edwin Mellen Press, 1992), p. 66.
46. Although it was once common to conceal from adopted children the facts about their origins, psychologists and adoption experts now fully support the rabbis' ancient wisdom regarding honesty and openness.
47. To order this book, contact Resources for Adoptive Parents, 3381 Goreham Avenue, Minneapolis, MN 55426 (612-926-6959).
48. Rabbi Daniel Shevitz, "A Guide for the Jewish Adoptive Parent," *Response* 48 (Spring) 1985.
49. The prayer for a son is based on the words of the patriarch Jacob, spoken when he acknowledged his two grandsons, Menashe and Ephraim, the sons of Joseph and Asenath, his Egyptian wife (Genesis 48:1–21). The prayer for a daughter is from the Book of Ruth.

PART IV: *Celebrating Conversion*

✦

Conversion Celebrations

1. Since conversion is not one of the 613 *mitzvot* enumerated in the Bible, the term *s'eudat mitzvah* is not technically apt; *s'eudat simcha* is an alternative.
2. Mazon asks American Jews to contribute this fraction of all life-cycle celebration costs to help feed the hungry in the United States and abroad, Jews and non-Jews alike. Mazon: 12401 Wilshire Boulevard, Suite 303, Los Angeles, CA 90025-1015 (310-442-0020).

Tzedakah

3. Leviticus 111.
4. Danny Siegel, *Gym Shoes and Irises* (Spring Valley, N.Y.: Town House Press, 1982), pp. 120–24.
5. Keritot 9:1.
6. Pirke Avot 1:14.
7. Rambam, Mishneh Torah, "Gifts to the Poor," 7:7.

8. Adapted from Danny Siegel, "19 Occasions for Giving Tzedakah," *Gym Shoes and Irises.*

Hiddur Mitzvah: Making It Beautiful

9. Thanks to Cantor Jennifer Worby for letting me read her master's thesis, "A Modern Musical Conversion Ceremony," which includes many more ideas and songs, and for our informative conversation about conversion and the cantorate. Thanks also to Cantors Robert Scherr and Roy Einhorn for their comments and suggestions.

10. "Sing unto God," "Lechi lach," and "The promise" by Debbie Friedman (Sounds Write); "Entreat me not" by Lawrence Avery (Transcontinental Music Publications); "Song of Ruth" by Maurice Goldman (Transcontinental Music); "May God inspire" by Myrna Cohen (Sounds Write); "Ashreinu" by Sidney Hodkinson (Transcontinental Music); "Adonai oz" by Jeff Klepper (JESR—Jewish Educators for Social Responsibility); "May you live to see your world fulfilled" by Benjie Ellen Schiller (Transcontinental Music); and "V'erastich li" by Ben Steinberg (Transcontinental Music).

   This catalog of songs is intended only to suggest the use of music in conversion rituals and ceremonies.

11. From Danny Siegel, *Unlocked Doors* (1983).

12. From Marge Piercy, *Or Chadash (P'nai Or Siddur)* (Middlemarsh, 1989).

13. This meditation appears in *Siddur Birkat Shalom,* published by the Havurat Shalom Siddur Project, Somerville, Massachusetts, 1993.

14. From Danny Siegel, *A Hearing Heart* (1982).

15. From Edmund Flegg, *Why I Am a Jew* (New York: Bloch Publishing Co., 1945).

16. From *Voices Within the Ark,* ed. Howard Schwartz and Anthony Rudolf (New York: Avon, 1980).

17. From Danny Siegel, *A Hearing Heart.*

A Word About Weddings

18. Thanks to Shirley Waxman, fabric artist extraordinaire.

19. For more about how to be the architect of your own wedding, see *The New Jewish Wedding* by Anita Diamant (New York: Simon & Schuster, 1987).

20. Some rabbis and cantors require that those who participate under the *huppah* be Jews.

21. Thanks to calligrapher Elaine Adler for her insight and information.

22. The reason for this practice is to conform to the Jewish law that prohibits the marriage of a male *kohane,* or member of the priestly class, to a convert. Priests are not permitted to marry widows and divorcées either.

23. Brenda Forster and Rabbi Joseph Tabachnik, *Jews by Choice: A Study of Converts to Reform and Conservative Judaism* (Hoboken, N.J.: Ktav 1991), p. 49.

24. This tends to happen not because a parent's death gives permission but due to a realization that you wish your own death to be marked by Jewish burial, funeral, and mourning rites.

PART V: *Becoming Jewish*

Creating a Jewish Identit—
Living a Jewish Life

1. Yevamot 48b. In traditional parlance, this is mostly a legal—rather than a spiritual or psychological—metaphor and is applied to such matters as laws of inheritance, testifying in court, etc.

2. Sholem Aleichem was the pseudonym of Yiddish author and humorist Sholem Rabinowitz (1859–1916).

3. David Patterson, *Pilgrimage of a Proselyte: From Auschwitz to Jerusalem* (Middle Village, N.Y.: Jonathan David Publishers, 1993), p. 119.

4. See *The Intermarriage Handbook: A Guide for Jews and Christians* by Judy Petsonk and Jim Remsen (New York: William Morrow, 1988) for further citations on ethnotherapy.

Your Mitzvot

5. Abraham Joshua Heschel, *God in Search of Man: A Philosophy of Judaism* (New York: Farrar, Straus and Giroux, 1955), p. 297.

6. According to Mishnah Pe'ah 1: "These are the obligations without measure, whose reward, too, is without measure: To honor mother

and father, to perform acts of loving-kindness, to attend the house of study daily, to welcome the stranger, to visit the sick, to rejoice with the bride and bridegroom, to comfort the bereaved, to pray with sincerity, to make peace when there is strife. And the study of Torah is equal to them all because the study of Torah leads to them all."

7. Pirke Avot, chap. 1.

Your Torah

8. Julius Lester, *Lovesong: Becoming a Jew* (New York: Henry Holt and Co., 1988), p. 175.

9. Barry Holtz, *Back to the Sources: Reading the Classic Jewish Texts* (New York: Summit Books, 1984), p. 12.

10. Actually, there are others present at the table, too, because when Jews gather to study Torah, it's common to invoke the opinions of great rabbis and exegetes of the past, some of whose ideas appear in the *humash*, the book used to study the weekly Torah readings. Akiva, Shammai, Hillel, and Eliezer from the Talmudic period, Rashi, Nachmanides, Rashbam, and Ibn Ezra from the Middle Ages: these teachers and others continue to provide startling insights into the text and shape contemporary questions and debates.

11. The body of literature called the Midrash actually contains two distinct streams: law (*halachah*) and stories (*aggadah*). *Midrash halachah*—the search for law—was how the rabbis interpreted God's expectations with respect to Jewish behavior. Thus, *kashrut*—the system of rules governing what and how Jews eat—was elaborated from a few lines in the book of Leviticus and other references to food in the Torah.

12. Rabbinic *midrash* flourished between 400 and 1200 C.E. See the chapter "Midrash" in Holtz, *Back to the Sources.*

13. Norman J. Cohen, *Self, Struggle and Change: Family Conflict Stories in Genesis and Their Healing Insights for Our Lives* (Woodstock, Vt.: Jewish Lights Publishing, 1995), p. 15.

14. The Torah says nothing explicit about the bond between Terah and Abraham. (His mother's name is not recorded.) There is no mention of filial love or conflict between Terah and his oldest son. However, in one of the most famous stories from midrashic literature, Terah is described as an idol manufacturer whose visionary son smashes his fa-

ther's goods and persuades other idolaters to follow the one true God. Terah and Abraham are presented as theological opposites: Terah represents the pagan world of idolaters, while Avram, the servant of Adonai, flees from his enraged father's house, having burned his bridges and repudiated his father's world view.

The rabbis cast this rupture in theological language, but there are other stories and different explanations to be read between the lines, such as the one given here.

15. Genesis 11:27. This and all translations from the Torah are taken from *The Five Books of Moses: The Schocken Bible*, vol. 1, A New Translation with Introductions, Commentary and Notes by Everett Fox (New York: Schocken Books, 1995). The Fox translation is intended to give the English reader a sense of the language and grammar of the original Hebrew.

16. Genesis 11:32, 21:1.

Community Matters

17. The word "synagogue" is not Hebrew, but appeared in the Christian Bible as the Greek translation of the term *beit k'nesset,* "house of assembly." Until the eighteenth century, Jews used the word "temple" only to refer to the original Temple in Jerusalem, which would, according to tradition, be rebuilt by divine command. The Reform movement rejected the notion of a rebuilt temple and used the word as a synonym for "synagogue." Some Conservative congregations are also called temples. *Shul,* meaning "school," is the Yiddish word for "synagogue."

PART VI: *Your History: A Short History of Conversion to Judaism*

1. Danny Siegel, "Statement by a Woman Who Has Chosen to Be a Jew." The poem appears in full in the chapter "*Hiddur Mitzvah: Making It Beautiful.*"

2. At the Friday night Shabbat dinner table, parents recite a blessing over their children. For boys, it is "May God make you as Ephraim and Menashe." See Anita Diamant with Howard Cooper, *Living a Jewish Life* (New York: HarperCollins, 1991), pp. 46–48, for more on this custom.

3. Rabbi Yose ben Halafta, a rabbi of the second century C.E., is described as a descendant of Jonadab son of Rechab. The Rechabites were an ascetic tribe that the Midrash later connected to the Sanhedrin.

    According to the Bible, Philistines, Ammonites, Sidonites, Hittites, Hurites, Calebites, Rechabites, Kenites, and Kenizzites joined the Israelite tribe in good faith. The exception that seems to prove the normative nature of conversion is the case of the Gibeonites, whose conversion was challenged as self-serving. See Joshua 9.

4. The Moabites are said to have been descended from the incestuous relationship between Lot and his daughters (Genesis 19:31–38). The prohibition against marrying Moabites is found in Deuteronomy 23:4–5.

5. Exodus 12:38.

6. The meaning of the word *ger* changed over time, from "foreigner" (in the Bible) to "resident alien" to, later still, "convert."

7. Joseph R. Rosenbloom, *Conversion to Judaism: From the Biblical Period to the Present* (Cincinnati: Hebrew Union College Press, 1978), p. 15.

8. Lawrence J. Epstein, *The Theory and Practice of Welcoming Converts to Judaism* (Dyfed, Wales: Edwin Mellen Press, 1992), p. 63.

9. David Max Eichhorn, ed., *Conversion to Judaism: A History and an Analysis* (Hoboken, N.J.: Ktav, 1965), p. 36.

10. The "Oral Torah" is traditionally defined as the laws and teachings handed down by those who received the written Torah on Mount Sinai, given by them to the elders and the rabbis and passed on in every generation until it was codified as the Talmud.

11. Babylonian Talmud, Shabbat 31a.

12. Hillel did not, however, prevail in all matters. The school of Hillel decreed that a circumcised convert needed to do nothing more regarding the covenant. Shammai, however, wanted a drop of blood to seal the covenant, and his opinion became law.

13. Tanchuma Buber, Lech Lecha 6, 32a.

14. Pesachim 87b.

15. The theological position that being a Jew was not a precondition for redemption or salvation explains why Judaism, unlike Christianity and Islam, never became a world-conquering religion.

16. Midrash Tanhuma.

17. Isaiah 56:3-7.

18. Norman Golb, *Jewish Proselytism: A Phenomenon in the Religious History of Early Medieval Europe* (University of Cincinnati Press, Rabbi Louis Feinberg Memorial Lecture, 1987), p. 34.

19. Rosenbloom, *Conversion to Judaism,* p. 176.

20. The tradition of conversion among clergy continues in the modern era: Abraham Carmel, who was ordained a Roman Catholic priest in Great Britain in 1943, converted to Judaism in 1954 and wrote a book about his life called *So Strange My Path* (New York: Bloch Publishing Co., 1964).

21. Rosenbloom, *Conversion to Judaism,* p. 83. There are many, many stories about converts. These are offered only as a sampling.

22. "Proselytes," *Encyclopaedia Judaica* (New York: Keter, 1971), vol. 13, p. 1187.

23. Midrash Rabbah II:16. Eichorn, ed., *Conversion to Judaism,* p. 84.

24. "Letter to Obadiah the Proselyte," in *A Maimonides Reader,* ed. Isadore Twersky (New York: Behrman House, 1972), pp. 475–76.

25. "The Prepared Table" was a practical guide to Jewish law written in the sixteenth century by Rabbi Joseph Karo in Safed, Palestine. It provided contemporary explications of the Talmud's position on matters of everyday importance, and remains an important source to this day.

26. Yoreh Deah, chap. 268.

27. Epstein, *Theory and Practice,* p. 131.

28. Ibid.

29. The 1990 National Jewish Population Survey turned up a few interesting statistics about converts and conversion. For instance, of the 185,000 people who call themselves Jews-by-choice, only 70 percent underwent a formal conversion; the other 30 percent simply live as Jews and consider themselves Jewish.

30. Lawrence J. Epstein, *Conversion to Judaism: A Guidebook* (Northvale, N.J.: Jason Aronson, 1994), p. 38.

AFTERWORD: *Kavod Ha-Ger: Honoring the Convert*

1. Mechilta.
2. Rabbi Mark Dov Shapiro, Sinai Temple, Springfield, Massachusetts.

About the Author

Anita Diamant, who is married to a Jew-by-choice, is the author of *The New Jewish Wedding, The New Jewish Baby Book, Living a Jewish Life, Bible Baby Names,* and a novel, *The Red Tent.* Her articles have appeared in the *Boston Globe Magazine, Parenting Magazine, Parents, McCall's, Reform Judaism,* and *Hadassah Magazine.* She lives in Newton, Massachusetts, with her husband and daughter.

BUILD YOUR JEWISH LIBRARY WITH

Schocken Books

What Do Jews Believe?
The Spiritual Foundations of Judaism
by David Ariel
0-8052-1059-8

On Judaism by Martin Buber
Foreword by Rodger Kamenetz
0-8052-1050-4

Saying Kaddish
How to Comfort the Dying,
Bury the Dead, and Mourn as a Jew
by Anita Diamant
0-8052-1088-1

The Five Books of Moses
The Schocken Bible, Vol. I
Translated with Introductions, Commentary and Notes by Everett Fox
0-8052-4140-X Standard Edition

Entering Jewish Prayer
A Guide to Personal Devotion and the Worship Service
by Reuven Hammer
0-8052-1022-9

Jewish Meditation A Practical Guide,
by Aryeh Kaplan
0-8052-1037-7

The Jewish Festivals
A Guide to Their History and Observance
by Hayyim Schauss
0-8052-0937-9

Available at your local bookstore, or call toll-free:
1-800-733-3000 (credit cards only).